Main Force to Mosquito Master Bomber

Main Force to Mosquito Master Bomber

The Story of Wing Commander Eric Benjamin DFC & Bar

By

Jeannie Benjamin and Sean Feast

Dedication by Jeannie Benjamin

'To my parents, Eric and Betty'

Published in 2024 by Fighting High Ltd
www.fightinghigh.com

Copyright © Fighting High Ltd, 2024
Copyright text © Sean Feast, 2024
Copyright text © Jeannie Benjamin, 2024

The rights of Sean Feast and Jeannie Benjamin to be identified as the authors of this book are asserted in accordance with the Copyright, Patents and Designs Act 1988.

The print publication is protected by copyright. Prior to any prohibited reproduction, storage in a retrieval system, distribution or transmission in any form or by any means, electronic, mechanical, recording or otherwise, permission should be obtained from the publisher.

The ePublication is protected by copyright and must not be copied, reproduced, transferred, distributed, leased, licensed or publicly performed or used in any way except as specifically permitted in writing by the publisher, as allowed under the terms and conditions under which it was purchased, or as strictly permitted by applicable copyright law. Any unauthorised distribution or use of this text may be a direct infringement of the authors' and the publisher's rights and those responsible may be liable in law accordingly.

British Library Cataloguing-in-Publication data. A CIP record for this title is available from the British Library.

ISBN – 13: 978-1838068745

Designed by Fighting High.

Printed and bound in Wales by Gomer Press.
Front cover design by Michael Lindley.

Contents

Foreword	vii
Preface	ix
Chapter One: Early Days	1
Chapter Two: A Glorious Month for Flying	9
Chapter Three: Saying Boo to an Alligator	25
Chapter Four: Thundering Through the Clear Air	45
Chapter Five: A Third Ring, A Baby, A DFC and a Bar	71
Chapter Six: Master Bomber	87
Afterword	117
Endnotes	127
Index	131

Eric Benjamin. Proudly sporting his new moustache.

Foreword

By Jeannie Benjamin

After our mother Betty was killed in a car crash in 1991 my sister and I had the unenviable task of sorting out the contents of her bungalow. It was while we were involved in this that we came across a shoe box in her wardrobe containing a bundle of letters, still inside their envelopes, and tied up with a blue ribbon. Carefully untying the ribbon and opening the envelopes, we were not surprised to find letters from our father Eric, written to our mother while he was based at various RAF stations during the Second World War. We had been aware of the existence of these letters as our mother had often spoken to us about them and quoted from them, so we did not feel we were intruding by reading them ourselves.

These letters are a testament to the love that our parents had for each other, set against a background of one of the fiercest wars in history, revealing a mixture of joy and longing, of the small everyday worries, and the desperate anxieties of wartime. This precious box of letters, kept so carefully for the then forty-six years since her husband had been shot down and killed, also testify to the continuing devotion our mother felt towards him.

In using these letters as the backbone for this book I have attempted to build up a picture of a man my sister and I scarcely knew. I was a toddler of eighteen months when he was killed and she was a baby of only three weeks. The letters which survive are considerable in number, thirty-six in all, but they do not cover the whole of the war period; they date from February 1943 to February 1945, when his life ended. Consequently, I have used other sources to obtain extra information. Unfortunately, my father's Log Book has not survived but I have scrutinised his Service Record, which was sent to me from the RAF and I have used family resources and photo albums as well as visiting the National Archives at Kew. I have also been grateful to various contacts on social media for supplying me with further details.

While there is no surviving correspondence from my mother to my father during those war years, I have nevertheless been able to use other letters which she wrote to her family and friends, both during that time and after he was killed, as well as letters she received from friends and officialdom. My mother also wrote a short memoir in her later years, and I have used parts of this. Other letters from my father do survive; they include those he wrote to his uncle and aunt in Canada and to the man who would become his brother-in-law, the husband of one of my mother's sisters.

Some explanation of the names of the people in the letters is required. My father's name was Eric Arthur Benjamin and Eric was the name he was known by among his family and friends. However, when writing to my mother he always used the name John. This was the name they used privately but she referred to him as Eric when writing to her friends and family. I grew up knowing this, but I do not remember ever hearing an explanation as to why they both used this name privately. I do know however that if I had been born a boy I would have been given the name John. (Incidentally John was also the name of my father's last navigator, who died with him.) Other names my father was known by more obviously within his squadrons were Benny and Benjy. My mother's name was Margaret Elizabeth Barry, but her family and my father always called her Bet or Betty. My father's mother and the rest of his family, however, always referred to her as Margaret, as did my father when writing to them.

Eric Arthur Benjamin was one of around 55,573 members of Bomber Command killed in the Second World War and each of course has his own story. In this semi-epistolary account of my father's life and death I have not attempted to tell the story of the war as it played out nationally and internationally; I have tried to paint a picture of one man's part within that war as he lived and loved at a time of enormous disturbance. I hope that the use of my father's very personal and poignant letters, which can only be called 'love letters', will be seen as a way of honouring the life of a man who simply wanted to learn to fly so that he could save up to get married and who was caught up in one of the most difficult periods in our history.

Preface

At 13.30hrs on Monday, 19 February 1945 the twenty-five-year-old Wing Commander, Eric Arthur Benjamin, a Master Bomber attached to No. 5 Group, sat down in his room at the Headquarters of No. 54 Base, RAF Coningsby, Lincolnshire to write a letter to his wife Betty.

> Hullo My Love, I thought I must drop you a line, now, as I felt like it. Before I tell you about the journey, etc., I want to say it was a simply beautiful leave – so complete with you and our children – he! It's so difficult to leave you, though. That last two minutes is awful, isn't it? Still, we mustn't dwell on it. I'm back on the job, again and we must get used to writing letters and looking forward to next time.
>
> I made very good time and got to Peterborough at 7.00 where I had a nice supper of plaice and veg. I made the camp at 9.15, which was very good going, wasn't it? I had to pay the Mess a visit and buy a round, of course, to celebrate. I turned in at 11.00 and had a good night. The baby didn't cry – or did she?
>
> I found a letter from Desmond in the wrack – just to say how do. In fact, here it is, which please return. Yes, I did forget my pipe and baccy! I thought I had it in my pocket. I expect you're sending it. Tell Pop that Dresden was hit really hard just as the newspapers and Jerry say. He was wanting to know. The Russians will be able to go forward again, now!
>
> Every bit of my love, Angel, to you and quite a bit for those kids of ours! Your John. xxxxxxx.

It was to be the last letter he would ever write. Seven years earlier, the eighteen-year-old Eric had written to his aunt and uncle in Canada. He had just joined the Royal Air Force Volunteer Reserve (RAFVR). 'At weekends,' he wrote, 'I am instructed into becoming a pilot. I think there is no greater sport than flying.'

Eric Benjamin, the fourth child of Albert and Beatrice.

Chapter One

Early Days

On 27 June 1919, the assistants and functionaries to the heads of the Big Four nations, David Lloyd George, Vittorio Orlando, Georges Clemenceau, and Woodrow Wilson, were putting the finishing touches to the document that would become famous the next day as the Treaty of Versailles. Almost seven months after the guns of the western front had finally fallen silent, the Allies had at last agreed on the terms of the peace, and the reparations due to the Entente powers, and were preparing to sign the document in the opulent splendour of the royal palace that gave the treaty its name.

Some 300 miles away at Eastbank Road in Hampton, Middlesex, Albert and Beatrice Benjamin were welcoming the arrival of their fourth child, a boy, who they named Eric Arthur. Eric was fortunate to have an older sister, Victoria, later known as 'Queenie', eleven years his senior, and two older brothers Albert (born 1909) and Leslie (born 1917). They were to be joined by the youngest child and another boy, Ernest, when Eric was three. To Queenie, the only girl, Eric was always her favourite brother.

The surname Benjamin betrays the family's proud Jewish heritage; Eric's grandfather was called Moses, his great-grandfather was Elias and his great-great-grandfather was another Moses. There were many uncles, aunts and cousins with popular Jewish names including Solomon, David and Sarah. His childhood was fairly typical of working-class families at that time. His father worked as a photographer for Hawker Aircraft in Kingston and used his skills to take a number of family photographs, spending long hours in his dark room at home developing and printing them. His mother was a housewife, by all accounts looking after the family and the home with great diligence.

Eric attended the local primary school and gained a place at Hampton Grammar School where he won at least one prize, a heavy tome entitled *Routledge's Universal Encyclopaedia*. The inscription placed inside the front cover reads: 'Prize awarded to E.A. Benjamin for 1st Prize, Form 5B' and bears the school motto Praestat Opes Sapientia - Wisdom Surpasses Wealth.

The three younger brothers, Eric, Ernest and Leslie enjoyed the outdoor life and became active in the Hampton Hill Sea Scouts, the Mountbatten Crew, from a young age. The Group, known affectionately as 'Skip's Boys', according to the wife of Skipper Percy Yaeldon, had an old Thames Sailing Barge called 'Venture' which had been converted into a floating headquarters and was moored at Hampton. The boys regularly went camping with the Sea Scouts in the summer while their parents went away to holiday on the coast.

There were two upsets in Eric's early life to disrupt an otherwise happy childhood. The first happened when he was eight years old. His sister Queenie, at the age of eighteen, fell in love with an older married man, Alec Turner. This caused a great deal of friction within the family and led to frequent and increasingly violent arguments between Eric's sister and their father. Eric, along with ten-year old Leslie, had the misfortune of witnessing one particular argument in which their father threatened Queenie with a carving knife. Only the brave intervention of his mother, standing between husband and daughter, prevented the situation from escalating further. Soon afterwards Queenie left home and went to live with her grandmother and Aunt Rose, their mother's younger sister, at Addlestone, near Weybridge in Surrey. Queenie was banished from her parents' lives and barely spoken of thereafter. She later became pregnant and gave birth to a daughter Sylvia in 1942, a second daughter Joan in 1944 and subsequently married the man she loved. In those less tolerant times, she was the black sheep of the family.

The second upset occurred when Eric was fifteen. His older brother Albert, (also known as Jerry) a keen motorcyclist, was killed in a road accident on 9 October 1934, the day after his twenty-fifth birthday. His death was keenly felt by Eric, who referred to the incident four years later in a Christmas letter written to his Uncle Arthur in Canada:

> It is terribly sad, to think that he was taken from life at such an early stage. We pray that his soul may rest with God, for he was always the life and soul of our family, especially at Christmas time.

These were to prove strangely prophetic words as Eric would himself be taken from life at an early stage: ten years later at the age of twenty-five, exactly the same age as his brother.

Eric left school at sixteen to work as a clerk at London Universal Insurance Company in the City of London. Two years later, in the spring of 1937, he met Margaret Elizabeth Barry, known as Betty or Bet to her family. Betty was the eldest daughter of Sarah and Stephen Barry, and of Irish heritage. Stephen's father was born in County Cork, and when he died Stephen had to abandon his mining engineer studies to become a coal miner in South Wales in order to provide for his mother and seven sisters. There he met Sarah Gurney, a Baptist, and married her when he was twenty-six and she seventeen, much to the dismay of his family who were all staunch Catholics.

Betty had an older brother, Desmond, and two younger sisters, Winnie and Claudia. They spent their early years in the small village of Aberbeeg. Money was tight and the Welsh tradition very strong. Stephen's forceful mother had all her son's children baptised as Catholics and sent them to boarding school in Hereford and then to St Albans where Stephen worked as a petrol pump attendant. Stephen and Sarah eventually obtained a council house at 23 Mays Road, Teddington, not far from Hampton, and Stephen became the proprietor of a small petrol station. They were a very close-knit family and all three girls were renowned wherever they went for their splendid auburn hair.

Betty described her first meeting with Eric in a memoir she wrote many years later:

> I met my handsome Sea Scout when I was 19, he 18. I can still remember my first sight of him striding along Teddington High Street in his Sea Scout uniform, just back from camping, all tanned and scrubbed and fit.

The courtship of Eric Benjamin and Betty Barry was a very innocent one, as Betty described in her memoir:

> Courting walks in Bushy Park every evening, such simple pleasures – mild snogging in the sitting room, shared with two sisters doing the same.

On the morning of Thursday, 15 September 1938, they went cycling together in Bushy Park. On that very same day the British Prime Minister Neville Chamberlain was visiting Adolf Hitler at Berchtesgaden, home of Hitler's famous mountain retreat known as the 'Eagle's Nest'. The guns of war were looming in the distance while Eric and Betty, like many young couples of the time, were enjoying the innocence of youth.

Despite being a Sea Scout, Eric's real passion was to fly. Not long after meeting Betty, in November 1937, Eric was attested into the Royal Air

Force Volunteer Reserve (RAFVR) as No.740801 Aircraftman 2nd Class/ Under Training Pilot (AC2 u/t pilot). The RAFVR gave young men between the ages of eighteen and twenty-five a chance to fly, or to train as an observer or wireless operator, while still in full-time employment. Its purpose was to supplement the Royal Auxiliary Air Force, the 'active' reserve, and enable an additional 'non-active reserve' of aircrew to be created to draw upon in the event of war. The Air Ministry principally drew upon civilian assets, especially private flying clubs and the increasing number of commercial operators, to provide what support they could by way of training, and so it was that Eric reported to White Waltham, near Maidenhead, to commence his flying instruction on 25 September 1938. White Waltham was a civilian airfield which had been built by the de Havilland family ten-years earlier as the home of the de Havilland Flying School. By the time Eric arrived, the airfield had been taken over by the British Government, and soon after became the home airfield for the Air Transport Auxiliary (ATA), an eclectic band of often older men and daredevil women who delivered the aircraft direct from the factories to the front-line squadrons.

While Eric began his elementary flying training, the British Prime Minister, Neville Chamberlain, was seeking to assure a sceptical British public that there would be 'Peace in our time', despite the sinister machinations of a new Nazi Germany. Chamberlain returned from a conference in Munich, landing just up the road from Eric in Heston, famously holding aloft a piece of paper stressing the importance of Anglo-German relations and expressing the 'desire of our two peoples never to go to war with one another again'.

Eric's motivation for joining the RAFVR, as much as the thrill of flying, was to save a little extra money through his flying pay to enable him to get married. Promoted sergeant, his training progressed well, and his peers deemed him to be of 'very good' character.

During the happy spring and nervous summer of 1939 Eric and Betty continued to enjoy many happy hours and days of courtship. It was not long before Eric proposed to Betty, and she accepted. They managed to spend a few days together in places as far away as Shipley in Yorkshire and Jaywick Sands in Essex. In April Betty celebrated her twenty-first birthday and in June Eric reached the age of twenty. In the second week of August, they holidayed on the Isle of Wight, which Eric referred to as 'The Garden Isle'. Betty made reference to those happy times in her memoir:

> We went on holiday together to the Isle of Wight. We were given adjoining rooms and only used the one bed, snuggled up together but positively no hanky panky. Where is the innocence of yesteryear?

During their week away war was growing ever closer. On 7 August a secret meeting took place at Schleswig-Holstein between some British businessmen and Hermann Göring in a last-ditch but ultimately futile effort to avoid war.

On Saturday 2 September 1939, Eric, handsome, fresh-faced, and clean-shaven, was recalled from the reserve and mobilised. In his case it meant more formal training into the ways of service life with a short course at No. 3 Initial Training Wing (ITW). ITW was an eight-week 'right of passage' through which all trainee aircrew were obliged to pass. At ITW, the men were divided into 'Flights' (A, B, C or D) and a Squadron, and training effectively split into two parts: classroom work and physical exercise. For the former, aircrew were obliged to study specific subjects such as mathematics, navigation, armaments, signals and aircraft recognition, as well as topics such as Air Force Law. Health and personal hygiene also featured. Outside of the classroom and there were endless periods of 'square bashing', learning how to march properly and salute smartly, and sport. Sport was primarily swimming (3 ITW was based at St Leonards-on-Sea) and long-distance running.

Eric passed ITW easily enough and in the second week of October was posted to No. 7 Service Flying Training School (SFTS) in Peterborough to extend his flying experience with more complicated aircraft and manoeuvres. Whereas his basic flying training had been on the ubiquitous DH82 Tiger Moth in a series of basic drills over a dozen or so hours until they went 'solo' for the first time, now he was flying more powerful aircraft with more sophisticated systems. Again he didn't struggle, and was awarded his coveted 'wings' with a pass of 78%.

While in the middle of his SFTS course, sitting quietly in the Sergeants' Mess in a rare moment to himself, Eric wrote to Alf Lock, the boyfriend of Betty's sister Claudia and who would later become Claudia's husband. In his letter he reveals something of the banality and frustrations of wartime training.

> Dear Alf,
> It's a sod having to repeat news over and over to each one I write to, but, blast it, here goes:
> Things generally are bloody comfortable (having my last curses and swears as a bachelor, so pass it). There's no rationing here and not much likelihood of it. In the Mess we are waited on hand and foot, and out of the Mess, though we are certainly not waited on, there are no 'Army' orders or such like, but we are politely told 'to do a certain thing' (of

course, if we don't do it – that's another question!).

The C.F.I. (Chief Flying Instructor) feels his bloody weight! He's cancelled all leave till the end of this intermediate eight-week course. That's got our backs up and we threatened (behind closed doors and keeping a watchful eye at the window) to 'do something about it' – God only knows what – but there you are, wouldn't you have felt the same? Eight damn weeks without a break (unless our backs break under the strain) – it's too much to ask of any reasonable chap.

In the dim past, I seem to recollect such happy things as (I think we called them) – 'week-ends'. Every day here is almost exactly similar, so God knows when we come to a 'week-end', - there is no week-end. Each day we get up, eat, drill for about an hour, fly, attend lectures, eat, attend lectures, fly, eat and go to bed; and that happens every day, so where's the week-end? But I must confess the whole programme is very interesting, though tiring.

Eric's letter reveals something of the hazards of flying in a country now on an active war footing:

When flying, we must keep 10 miles away from the coast or 'certain unidentified aircraft might be the subject of attention for certain anti-aircraft batteries'.

Also, unless we wish to become entangled amongst the network of a Balloon Barrage, we must not view Nottingham from the air. The country up here is of deep interest to all of us, being new to most. However, the interest of one of us went a little too far afield and on studying his map (we all carry one) he had not the faintest idea where he was! On landing in the farmer's field (unploughed, lucky for him) he discovered rabbit pie on the lunch menu and that he was a little south of Huntingdon (30 miles off). His instructor brought him back safely and told him not to do it again.

I saw more country at the same time the other day, than ever before. From 15,000 feet I could see The Wash – 40-50 miles away. This is an endurance test, as after 30 minutes at that height, the rarefied air makes one pant a bit. After sticking it out, the quickest way down is to drop the nose and spin (you come out of the spin in time, of course, with a bit of a giddy head).

Well, Alf old cock, I'm sorry to hear of the separation just at a time when I'm getting properly hitched, but maybe it's all for the best. You must forgive me for not writing earlier, but I've so much correspondence to keep up with. Shall be very glad to hear from you if you've got a moment.

EARLY DAYS

Meantime all the very best. Remember me to any clubites who had the pleasure of knowing me, and just put an end to this silly, futile war business.

Eric was excited at the thought of his upcoming marriage to Betty. The 'silly, futile war business' had accelerated their plans and the date for the wedding was set for Saturday 2 December at the Roman Catholic Church of The Sacred Heart and St Margaret Mary in Teddington, where Betty attended Mass every Sunday. It was five minutes' walk from the home where she lived with her parents and siblings. Betty was a practising Catholic and her family had a very strong faith. Eric had a strong belief in God and had been brought up a Protestant but had no issue with getting married in a Catholic church.

Betty was not at all bothered about the finer points of their wedding. The country was at war and all she wanted was to be married to her sweetheart. A traditional white wedding dress was of no interest and she chose, instead, a green dress to complement her beautiful long wavy auburn hair. Her two sisters were to be the bridesmaids. The day finally arrived and the excitement of the twenty-year-old groom and his twenty-one-year-old bride was palpable. The reception to be held at home after the ceremony was all prepared and everything was set. Then things started to go wrong.

Halfway through the morning Betty's youngest sister, seventeen-year-old Winnie, developed pains in her stomach. These pains rapidly became severe, and an ambulance was called. Winnie was rushed to hospital and diagnosed with peritonitis, a potentially life-threatening condition requiring immediate treatment. Her boyfriend Aubrey, whom she had met at the age of fifteen and who would later become her husband, accompanied her to the hospital and after the rest of the family had received reassurance that Winnie was out of danger they decided to go ahead with the wedding.

Delayed by the morning's upset they all arrived at the church an hour late for the ceremony. Bride, groom, parents, siblings, Sea Scouts and many friends were gathered, but of the Registrar there was no sign. At a Catholic wedding a civil registrar is required to be present so that after the religious ceremony the bride and groom can be legally married in the eyes of the State. The guests waited patiently until their patience was exhausted, and two of them set off to see if they could find where the registrar had got to. He could not be found. The registrar had made a mistake about the date.

Now the wedding party had a decision to make and opted to take the pragmatic route. Since the reception was ready, and the food had been prepared, they decided to press on with the celebrations even though no wedding had actually taken place! The wedding cake was duly cut, the health and future prosperity of the 'bride and groom' was toasted, photographs were taken and Eric and Betty each went back to their parental homes, spending the night apart. Somehow the national press got hold of the story and published pictures of the happy couple enjoying their 'wedding reception' despite not being married! The newspapers put all these setbacks down to the fact that Betty had worn a green dress to her wedding which was considered very bad luck. Headlines of 'Are You Superstitious?' and 'The Bride in Green – What Happened!' shouted from their pages.

Not to be deterred, Eric and Betty were married the following day, 3 December 1939, exactly three months after Neville Chamberlain had mournfully announced that the country was now at war. They enjoyed a week's honeymoon at Possingworth Park Hotel in Bournemouth, which Betty described later as an 'awful stuffy hotel, full of OAPs', saying she couldn't think why Eric had chosen the place. They were glad to get home to a lovely party prepared for them by Eric's mother.

The newly-weds began their married life living at Betty's parents' home at 23 Mays Road. Stephen and Sarah Barry were very happy to accommodate their daughter and her new husband, although the house was now somewhat crowded. Both Winnie and Claudia were still at home, and there were only three bedrooms. Soon, too soon, Eric's leave was over, and a more dangerous period in his life was about to begin.

Chapter Two

A Glorious Month for Flying

After a blissful and eventful few days' leave for the wedding and subsequent honeymoon, Eric resumed his flying training, still a sergeant pilot and still impressing his instructors with a 'very good' rating.

On 7 March he ditched his sergeant's stripes and NCO's uniform for something more tailored on his appointment to a commission, a single thin stripe on his sleeves denoting his promotion to pilot officer. In this rank, like hundreds before him, Eric was commissioned 'for the duration of hostilities' into the General Duties (GD) branch of the Royal Air Force Volunteer Reserve, and in the short-term 'on probation' until such time as his appointment was confirmed. This was achieved in short order, and Eric promoted again to the war substantive rank of flying officer, the single thin stripe replaced by a slightly thicker one.

In attaining a commission, Eric's service number changed. He was given the very singular RAF Service number of 77777, which he and Betty considered to be very lucky [1].

Now at the end of his flying training, and with his logbook duly signed by the Chief Flying Instructor at No. 7 SFTS, Eric progressed to the operational training unit (OTU) at RAF Benson in South Oxfordshire, the final stage in his journey to a front-line bomber squadron.

Eric's first action on arriving at Benson from the Wallingford railway station was to 'warn in' and sign the visitors' book. This was to enable the mess secretary to count his numbers for catering purposes and accommodation. He then reported to the mess secretary's office to be allocated a room, or in Eric's case a bed in a room, since all junior officers were obliged to 'double up' and share. The following morning, Eric checked in with the OTU adjutant and reported to the Chief Instructor, who seemed more interested in his dog than the freshly-promoted flying officer standing in front of him. Notwithstanding the CI's disinterest, Eric was allocated to a Flight and proceeded to be kitted out with his flying clothing, including a seat-type parachute. Although uncomfortable, as Eric explains in a later letter, it was more practical than the observer-type 'chutes which had to be clipped onto a harness and required a feat of dexterity on the ground, let alone in the sky, in an aircraft potentially hit, on fire and out of control.

With Benson, Eric struck lucky. Being a permanent RAF station, it had modern accommodation and sanitation. A far cry from the Nissen huts and boggy fields upon which many temporary stations would later be built as the war machine gathered momentum. Benson was the product of a major expansion programme by the RAF in the late 1930s to meet the emerging threat of Nazi Germany. Two squadrons arrived in April 1939, Nos 150 and 103, and both left in September of the same year to become part of the Advanced Air Striking Force (AASF) then being assembled in France. Coinciding with Eric's arrival, Benson had been designated No. 12 OTU under the command of Wilfred Dunn, a former sea-plane pilot whose mutton-chop whiskers made him instantly recognisable.

Benson gave Eric his first exposure to the aircraft he would fly operationally, an aircraft originally designed as a war winner but might better have been described as a widow maker: the Fairey Battle. The Battle, first flown in March 1936, promised great advances over the biplane light bombers it was destined to replace when it was chosen by the Air Ministry[2] to help equip the rapidly expanding RAF. A monoplane of clean design and of all-metal, stressed skin construction, it could carry twice as many bombs twice as far as the Hawker Harts and Hinds which had done such sterling service. Practice defensive formations flown before the war exposed the Battle's obvious weaknesses, prompting one experienced flight commander to describe it as little better than a flying coffin whose only chance of surviving fighter interception 'was to fly her on her bottom'.[3]

Speed was meant to be her strength, but in reality the Battle was underpowered and lacked both the performance and defensive fire power demanded by modern air weaponry. Its single Vickers K gun mounted in the open rear cockpit had a poor arc of fire, and for the gunner to fire abeam meant thrusting his body into the slipstream. There was also the possibility of damaging the tail fin, with no cut off device in the mid-line. The leading edge was reinforced so that should a bullet make contact, it would hopefully be deflected![4]

As a pure flying machine, however, the Battle was something of a delight, especially to those whose flying training had been on aircraft that wouldn't have looked out of place over the trenches in the first world war. Some of the New Zealand pilots under training at Benson took particular pleasure in putting the Battle through its paces, swooping and diving as though she were a fighter. The full complement of a Battle comprised a crew of three: pilot, observer and wireless operator/air gunner (Wop/Ag), all sitting line astern. It made for a very crowded cockpit, and the weight of the crew, along with a full bombload, made for a slow and laborious climb. It took more than four minutes to reach 5,000ft and more than twenty-one minutes to reach 20,000ft. (By contrast, the Spitfire II could do the latter in seven.)

Operational training included a series of cross-country exercises, often at low level, watching the sheep and cattle scatter in fear and surprise as the crews headed out for navigation or bombing practice, the latter on the Otmoor ranges close-by. Eric honed his dive-bombing skills, for in the Battle it was the pilot who aimed and dropped the bombs using a mark etched on his windscreen. There was also talk of high-level practice over Lough Neagh, soon abandoned as news began to filter through of the appalling losses suffered by the Battle squadrons in France in high-level sorties.

May was a glorious month for flying, but not so on the Continent. The inadequacy of the Fairey Battle, and the folly of unescorted daylight operations by light bombers, was quickly exposed. On 10 May, three-days before Eric received his movement orders to proceed to France, the Germans launched their main attack in the West, and the Allies were soon in disarray. Battles of No. 12 Squadron made their now-famous but ill-fated attack on the bridges at Maastricht, an attack in which two of their number were awarded the Victoria Cross, the first to be awarded to members of the RAF in the Second World War. Four days later, by which time Eric had been posted to No. 98 Squadron, an all-out effort by Battles of five separate squadrons to stop the German advance at Sedan led to the loss of forty out of an attacking force of seventy-one aircraft.

Prior to leaving for France, Eric collected his camp kit from the stores. Along with a heavy canvass bedroll containing his camp bed and washbasin, he also collected his webbing to which he attached a revolver (a .38 revolver drawn from the armoury), water bottle, and other accoutrements of a military nature including a small box of ammunition. He already had his gas mask which he was obliged to always carry other than when flying.

His posting to No. 98 Squadron, effective 13 May 1940, meant he was now under the umbrella of the British Air Forces in France (BAFF), a force established four months' earlier almost to the day. Under the command of Sir Arthur 'Ugly' Barratt, BAFF was intended to provide unified command of the RAF in France. There were in effect two parts to BAFF: the RAF component of the British Expeditionary Force (BEF) to provide direct support to troops on the ground, principally by way of tactical reconnaissance and photographic survey, and the AASF with much wider responsibilities. Commanded by 'Pip' Playfair, the AASF comprised ten squadrons of light bombers (Battles and twin-engine Bristol Blenheims) and two and later four squadrons of Hawker Hurricane fighters to protect the bombers and their landing grounds. In deploying the AASF in France, the original intention was to bring short-range bombers within striking distance of German industry. This intention was quickly replaced by the pragmatic and urgent need to support the armies on the ground who were, or soon would be, in full retreat from the German Blitzkrieg.

Eric's stay with No. 98 Squadron was short-lived. In essence, the squadron served as both a training unit and a reserve unit that acted as a replacement 'pool' for those other Battle squadrons in the front line, and on 25 May Eric was transferred to No. 150 Squadron at Pouan under the command of Allen Hesketh. 'Bill' Hesketh was typical of his generation, and several officers commanding frontline squadrons at the start of the war. At forty he was twice the age of many of the men under his command. He'd seen service at the tail end of the First World War as an observer when he had been wounded in action during a low-level reconnaissance sortie, recovering sufficiently to take part in the RAF's campaign in south Russia in 1919/20. While retraining as a pilot, he survived a crash in February 1922 in an Avro 504K which struck telegraph wires and then hit a tree just as it struggled to gain height after take-off. Hesketh escaped with slight injuries but Flight Lieutenant Robert Jenkins MBE MC, his instructor, fractured his skull and died. Later, he became a flight commander with No. 13 Squadron, an army co-operation unit, in 1933, and eventually OC No. 150 Squadron in March 1939. Not one to fly a desk, Hesketh led one of the squadron's first operations on 25 September and was shot up for his troubles! He was fortunate not to be flying five days later when the squadron lost five of their number in a single afternoon.

By the time of Eric's arrival, the squadron was all-but done in. Since the war began, they had lost twenty aircraft to enemy fighters (both single-engine Messerschmitt Bf109s and twin-engine Bf110 'Zerstorers' which equipped the Luftwaffe's front-line squadrons in 1940) or flak, or aircraft destroyed on the ground or through training accidents. They had, in short, suffered a 100% casualty loss, and most of them had come in the few short days in May.

On the day the AASF launched its all-out attack on the bridges and columns of troops in Sedan, No. 150 Squadron contributed four aircraft, and all four bombers were lost. Eleven of the twelve squadron aircrew were killed; one was captured and interned. It was a far cry from operations the month before, which had focused on dropping propaganda leaflets ('Nickels') on German cities close to the border. Although dangerous in their own right, and exposing the bombers to heavy flak, they had seemed almost genteel by comparison. Now the harsh realities of war were staring them hard in the face.

With the start of Operation Dynamo and the evacuation at Dunkirk, the writing was already well and truly on the wall. It was no longer a matter of if the end would come, it was just a question of when. The squadron had already abandoned the airfield at Ecury-sur-Coole which had been their home since arriving in France in favour of Pouan-les-Vallées, a rural commune in the Aube department of north-central France, and a little further to the south. Two weeks later it moved west again to Houssay, a point in the middle of a triangle between Le Mans, Tours and Orleans. Every move required the laborious process of packing essential kit and stores, all of which had to be transported by lorry, and what they couldn't carry they had to destroy. Groundcrew and aircrew alike slept in whatever accommodation they could find, in barns and bell tents, with little or nothing in the way of ablutions or home comforts. They were literally and metaphorically birds on a wing, keeping one-step ahead of the advancing Germans who had them in a stranglehold with no intention of loosening their grip.

By 10 June, France was dissolving into chaos. Barratt had taken the sensible option in withdrawing the AASF from the south Champagne to the region around Orleans and Le Mans in a brief lull before the German's second offensive. A day later, however, when the enemy broke through the French positions on the Marne, Oise and Seine, the last line upon which any meaningful resistance could be built, he recognised that every unit, No. 150 Squadron included, was in imminent danger. On 13 June, No. 150 Squadron lost another three aircraft in a single morning. Whereas over recent days, operating mainly at night, this was yet another daylight, and yet again exposed the vulnerabilities of the Battle to Luftwaffe fighters. Six men were killed or captured, and in the remaining Battle, the gunner was badly injured. His pilot and flight commander, Robert Bradley, did well to bring the seriously damaged aircraft down in one piece.

The Germans, however, did not always get things their own way. In the same raid on Thursday 13 June, the Wop/Ag within Sergeant Sydney Andrews' aircraft, Henry Figg, took on four Bf109s, and claimed to have shot one of the aircraft down. The Battle returned safely to base. Andrews, Figg, and their observer, Norman Ingram, were all awarded the DFM. In a raid on the following day, Robert Burrows, the air gunner within Flight Lieutenant Beale's crew emptied an entire pan of ammunition into a German fighter at only fifty-yards range and saw the aircraft disappear trailing black smoke.

With Paris falling to the Germans on 14 June and no conceivable justification for retaining a fighting force in France, Operation Aerial, the final evacuation of British troops from the country, was enacted, Barratt again skilfully marshalling his squadrons and defences around the key ports of Nantes and St Nazaire whence the flow of fighting and support troops would be heaviest. In the late afternoon of 14 May, No. 150 Squadron received orders to prepare to retreat to Nantes, and to send a small advance party to receive aircraft. The main party was to follow during the night. Later that same evening it received further orders to detail ten aircraft for a dawn reconnaissance and to bomb any troop concentrations or targets of interest around the areas of Louvieres, Vernon, Viry, Danville and Evreux. They were promised fighter protection.

Eric and his crew were one of the ten selected. It would be their first operation together, and as it happened, their last. As his regular observer, Eric had Sergeant Armstrong, a slight young man with an infectious smile. Behind Armstrong sat the air gunner who also operated the radio, Eric Hillyard, a man of considerable presence. As well as sharing a Christian name with Eric, Hillyard was also married.

The plan for the operation, such as it was, called for the small force to be sent out in pairs to harry the advancing enemy over an extended period and prevent the Battles from all being on the ground at the same time. Immediately after the operation, the aircraft were to be inspected, refuelled, and flown home to the UK. The first two pairs took off shortly after 0400hrs. Eric, in Fairey Battle L5541, with the letters JN-A on its fuselage, was the last to get away at 0510hrs, in the company of Charles 'Tiny' Elliott, a young pilot officer, in Battle L5592.

As the dawn broke, the two aircraft headed steadily for the area south of the Seine where German Wehrmacht columns had been reported. The air gunners were very much on the alert for any fighters, Hillyard constantly scanning the sky behind and to the beam. Their own cover was nowhere to be seen. The German ground troops, clearly aggrieved at their presence, greeted them with a wall of heavy flak. Seeing no sign of any troop movements, Eric decided to target the village from where most of the anti-aircraft fire appeared to be coming. He banked the aircraft to port and as he started to dive onto the target, and line up the enemy flak position in his sights, Hillyard shouted a warning and simultaneously opened fire. What he first hoped might be friendly Hurricanes or Hawk 75s were anything but: three Bf109s had spotted them; they swooped to attack.

Eric was at 4,000ft and immediately pushed the stick forward and dived for the ground, twisting and jinking by kicking the rudder bar to avoid the enemy fire while Hillyard continued to let loose short, sharp bursts as the Messerchmitts danced into range. Eric's Battle could manage 210 mph flat out, the fighters 100mph more, and despite gaining speed in the dive he was quickly overhauled. Now they were at the Germans' mercy. Machine gun and canon shells soon found their mark, bullets tearing into the cockpit, one narrowly missing Eric's head and grazing the top of his flying helmet.

In a fight for their lives, it was always going to be an uneven contest but somehow Eric managed to keep the enemy at bay long enough for them to either give up the fight or believe that he was done for. More bullets slammed into the rear of the aircraft, Eric hearing an agonised groan from his gunner as he was hit and seriously hurt, his arm hanging loosely, and blood seeping from a puncture wound in his side.

With his aircraft damaged and the controls not responding as they should, Eric had to think fast. Hillyard was bleeding heavily and needed urgent medical attention. His pilot had no option other than to force land. Now some 40km southwest of Dreux, near the village of La Ferté-Vidame, Eric eased the aircraft down and managed a textbook landing in a small field, the Battle rolling gently to a halt leaving a small groove of tyre tracks in the soft brown earth. The briefest moment of silence was followed by the quick evacuation of the aircraft, Eric and the observer lifting their wounded comrade gently from the damaged rear cockpit and onto the grass.[5]

By now quite a crowd of men, women and children had gathered, fascinated by the sight of a British aircraft, and Eric was able to organise a French ambulance for his wounded gunner, taking him to hospital in Le Mans. Eric knew the injury was serious but unlikely to be fatal. With Hillyard safely taken care of, Eric considered his options while the crowd looked on. The field was too small and the controls of the aircraft too damaged to attempt to take off. It still had its bombs on board, so the risk was too great. It also meant that they couldn't set it on fire. Reluctantly both pilot and observer set about smashing what they could of the controls and the engine to render the Battle useless to the enemy, and then started the long and arduous trek to the coast at Nantes at the mouth of the Loire.

It took Eric and his observer the better part of three days to make the journey, grabbing what transport they could when it was offered: an ambulance; a goods train; even a motorbike. But for long periods they walked across fields and along roads clogged with the detritus of refugees, a pitiful sight of broken carts, broken horses, broken people. Mothers with babes in arms; the elderly with what few possessions they could carry; soldiers of various nationalities and uniforms. The French Poilus mixed with the British Tommy, still with their kit and rifles. Retreating but not all with the look of defeat. All eager to make the relative safety of the coast, and the chance of a ship back to England. Occasionally a German aircraft would appear overhead, a marauding Messerschmitt or Junkers 88, the sound of their approach and the impending misery sending columns of terrified men, women and children diving for what cover they could find, a ditch, a tree, or sometimes just staring blindly, paralysed with fear. Not surprisingly there was the occasional outbreak of violence, raised voices and pushing and shoving leading to a fight, reflecting the chaos around them.

They finally arrived dirty, dishevelled, unshaven and exhausted to the great rambling Breton town of Nantes on the late afternoon of 17 June, only to find the aerodrome in the process of being abandoned. Unserviceable aircraft were being burned, vandalised, or cannibalised for parts; fuel reserves destroyed. A café on the corner of the airfield did its best to keep at least some of the men in coffee and sandwiches.[6] The town too had an air of decay. Eric's own unit, No. 150 Squadron, had already departed, and its Battles flown back to the UK. The groundcrews and administrative staff were following by sea.[7] As one war correspondent was later to write: 'I have never seen such a collection of aircraft. In one corner a number of French mechanics were filling the fuel tanks of Moranes, Curtiss fighters and Potez machines. Nearby were several French bi-planes of old design. The middle of the field was occupied by British aircraft. There were a number of Hurricanes (one without a rear wheel); one or two Battles which appeared to be unserviceable; Wellingtons; DH86s; a Flamingo; two of the big Ensigns; a Handley Page Harrow and a couple of Magisters. Dozens of RAF officers, pilots and ground staff were scurrying hither and thither, loading all sorts of equipment into the big transport planes.'[8]

Eric was lucky. On the field, abandoned, was a Bristol Bombay, an ancient high-winged monoplane that was new to the RAF as a bomber/troop carrier but with its ungainly appearance had the look of an aircraft from another age. While the Bombay's fuel tanks were full, Eric and his observer scrounged a space, grateful to be on their way home and safety. They were some of the very last to leave.[9] By the early afternoon of the following day, the first of the German mechanised forces arrived and the French began suing for peace and a formal Armistice. On 18 June, in London, the future French President Charles de Gaulle made his now famous Appeal: 'La France a perdu une bataille! Mais La France n'a pas perdu la guerre.' Perhaps more famously, Winston Churchill, the British Prime Minister, declared: 'If the British Empire and the Commonwealth lasts for a thousand years, men will still say 'This was their finest hour.''

Betty's sister Claudia described Eric's homecoming in a letter to her boyfriend Alf, who had joined the Army:

Well, Eric has got back from France. He arrived on Monday about midnight. Were we surprised! He had been travelling three days, consequently was very dirty (he hadn't had his clothes off for ages) and had grown a taz. It suits him too. He had to travel quite a way on the buffers of a train; there wasn't room inside, it was so crammed with refugees. He is alright, except for a swollen ankle, which was kicked by a refugee. From the things he was telling us he has had quite an exciting time. He had to make a forced landing as his rear gunner was shot, and so lost his squadron. He himself just missed a bullet, it grazed the top of his helmet. Really, it must be terrible out there. The pillaging that is going on. The French soldiers are stealing anything they can lay their hands on. Old Eric pinched a pair of socks, there were piles of things just dumped. He has got five quid's worth of francs, he didn't have time to change them in France and the bank won't change them here.

Honestly though, it was every man for himself. If Eric hadn't managed to fly home on Monday he might not have been able to get home at all. The hosts of planes they had to abandon because there weren't enough pilots to bring them home! They smashed as many as they could. Eric had to smash his, he couldn't burn it because he had some bombs in it. Just fancy, people are working day and night to make planes and they had to destroy so many. Good job he was able to get away. He and Bet are going away for a few days, he's got till next Monday.

Betty's own account of this, written much later in her memoir in 1991, is slightly different, but only in the way she incorrectly remembers how Eric flew home. The rest is a wonderful contrast of the shock and horror of war against the banalities of everyday life:

One of my most treasured memories is of the night of 17 June 1940 – the day France fell to the Germans. I awoke about 11.30pm to see my beloved husband of a few months, standing at my bedroom door – weary, dusty and with a sprained ankle, but full of joy at reaching home. He had arrived back at his aerodrome at Nantes after an early bombing raid that morning, to find the squadron had left hastily in the face of advancing Germans – my photograph the only thing left hanging on a tent pole. He jumped into a plane – a fighter, though he was a bomber pilot, and flew the channel! He crossed London on the underground, mingling with home going workers and arrived at 23 Mays Rd, Teddington, about 11.30pm.

This sounds incredible, but I so vividly remember his description of the utter chaos in France and the long lines of pathetic refugees he saw from the air and the contrast of the utter ordinariness of suddenly being among the London commuters on the underground.

What a rapturous reunion we had that night – I hadn't expected to see him for ages – was afraid he would have been taken prisoner as so many were. And the next morning he answered the doorbell to receive a telegram telling me he was missing. How we laughed!

A telegram authorised on 19 June by the Under Secretary of State at the Air Ministry was also sent to Eric's parents. It stated simply: 'Regret to inform you that your son, Pilot Officer Eric Arthur Benjamin is reported missing as a result of air operations on 15 June 1940. Should you receive news of him from any source please inform this department. His wife has also been informed.'

Albert Benjamin wrote to the Air Ministry by return, thanking them for their telegram and delighted in telling them that Eric was safe, and 'has returned from France and reported at Hendon'.

Betty's parents, Mam and Pop, gave up their double bed on the night of Eric's return for the newly-reunited couple to share. Eric was given a week's leave and he and Betty went away together for a few days.

Eric and Sergeant Armstrong reported to RAF Stradishall in Suffolk to rejoin their squadron on 24 June. Here they learned for the first time what had befallen some of their friends in escaping from France, and how some had got home, as the saying goes, 'on a wing and a prayer'. One pilot, Alan Frank, told of trying to take off to fly back to the UK only to suffer a dead engine. One of the ground crew had to clean the points with what he had, a screwdriver and a nail file. 'This would not have been acceptable in normal circumstances,' he said later, 'but one had to talk oneself into saying it was alright.' He navigated home with the help of a Michelin Guide.[10]

On balance the squadron had been lucky and celebrated their good fortune with a riotous party. Their fate could certainly have been worse. The sinking of the *HMT Lancastria*, the former ocean liner, off St Nazaire on 17 June wiped out almost an entire squadron. Ninety-six members of No. 98 Squadron, aircrew and groundcrew alike, perished in the tragedy.[11]

After the debacle in France, No. 150 Squadron was not required for operations for the remainder of the month and all aircrew and groundcrew granted four days' leave to rest and recover. Eric spent his leave in Teddington and was the hero of the hour among their small circle of friends who gathered to celebrate his twenty-first birthday on 27 June.

The following week, on 2 July and having returned to Stradishall, Eric took time to write to Alf, Claudia's boyfriend, with his own account of his escape from France:

It was bloody awful out in France - in every sense of the word - just bloody! Thank God I'm still alive! – But what fools were the pilots of the Messerschmitts who tried to shoot me down! Me, with a number like 77777! (did you know?). Me – a violent pacifist! Me, a Jew! Me, the husband of such a good, grand lady! The fools! But the pom-pom for my air-gunner – he was injured badly.

I don't feel in the mood to detail events out there, Alf, but it was a 'doubtful' life and I could have kissed the ground when I set foot once again on civilised (more or less) England. I only had five weeks out there, I know, but they were the hottest weeks since the outbreak. I was almost stranded with my observer when the BEF started doing a bunk. We went on a raid on 15 June and had to 'force-land' to get our air-gunner to hospital. The machine was almost unflyable and the field, anyway, too small to get out of, so we had a 200-mile journey across France – and no buses! We did it by foot, motor-bike, ambulance, refugee trains, goods trains and private cars! We travelled on the buffers of one train from 6-00pm till 4-00pm the following day! There wasn't room inside. We were of the last remnants of the RAF to leave, but we came home in style in a Bristol Bombay – a large troop-carrying aircraft.

I've had 10 days leave and tomorrow we'll be at the above address (RAF Station, Newton, Nottingham) doing Heaven-only-knows what! I'm at Stradishall, Suffolk at the moment. At Newton, Margaret and I hope to settle down. We're fed up with waiting. Anyway, - waiting for what? Peace? – God, what a wait! Am very tired, - must go to bed now.

Of Hillyard, it would be some time before Eric would learn of his fate. He had last seen his gunner being taken in an ambulance to hospital at Le Mans. The surgeons decided his right arm was so badly injured it had to be amputated, leaving him in much pain. The pace of the German advance was such that the medical staff were forced to abandon the hospital and relocate to Angers. On 18 June, however, the Germans reached and occupied Angers, cutting off any hope of escape.

While recuperating, Hillyard was regularly visited by two ladies, one Scottish and one Irish[12], who worked as governesses to two wealthy local French families. They agreed to help him escape and took advantage of a document Hillyard was given allowing him to leave the town under the terms of an ambiguous parole. When Hillyard learned in the middle of October that he was to be taken to a prison camp in Germany, his two accomplices took swift action, altered the dates on his documentation so he could travel without hindrance, and spirited him away.

They hid him for over a week, and then went by train to Tours where they arranged to meet a guide who would take the airman to

Bordeaux. On the way they learned that they could cross into the unoccupied zone at Bléré (France had by then been divided in two. One half occupied by the Germans and the other under the control of the French Vichy government). Like something out of a comedy, but with potentially deadly consequences, Hillyard was smuggled into the unoccupied zone on the back of a milk cart pulled by an old woman. He was then taken from farm to farm until a car could be arranged to drive him to Loches. A doctor re-bandaged his arm and directed him to the station to take a train to Marseille, but his journey was interrupted at Chateauroux where a French NCO put him up for the night in a hut full of French military men, also looking to escape capture. Eventually he reached Marseille and found himself in the care of a former Church of Scotland Minister, Reverend Caskie. Through Caskie, Hillyard's parents and his wife learned for the first time that their son and husband was alive, albeit badly injured. On 12 November, Hillyard attended a Medical Board at L'hopital Michel Lévy (a military hospital established in 1848) where he was granted an exit permit. On 27 December, more than six months after being shot down, he left Marseille for Gibraltar via Madrid. There he had to wait another six weeks until a passage home could be arranged, travelling in the company of an RAF NCO (Sergeant George Roskell) who was also now minus his right forearm, the result of an air attack on his aerodrome, and two French NCOs from L'armée de L'air.

Disembarking for England on the *MS Sobieski*, a polish passenger ship, the small party eventually arrived back in the UK at the port of Greenock on 23 February 1941. Hillyard was subsequently awarded a Mentioned in Despatches (MiD). The citation said his courage in escaping whilst still suffering from the effects of the amputation 'was highly commendable'.[13] Roskell, formerly of No. 226 Squadron, received the higher award of the Military Medal for his adventures and subsequent evasion.[14]

On 3 July Eric left Stradishall and moved with his Squadron in a convoy of motor coaches to RAF Newton in Nottinghamshire. There they joined No. 103 Squadron, coming under the command of No 1 Group. Two days later both squadrons were honoured by a visit from Arthur Barratt and 'Pip' Playfair who complimented them and thanked both air and ground staff for their work while serving with the AASF in France. They could not have done more, and the commanders had learned a good many lessons, for example, that accurate attack against small and well-defended targets was bound to be costly, particularly so when aircraft are called upon, as the Battles were, to do the work which infantry and artillery had failed to do. Night operations greatly reduced the losses, and although AASF was only at the beginning of its experience as a night flying force, there was great improvement in the casualty figures after 20 May.[15]

It was no surprise, therefore, that the men of No. 150 Squadron were ordered to further hone their skills with a comprehensive programme of night flying practice to ultimately complement the operations being undertaken by their heavy bomber colleagues. Penny packets of Battles also punctuated their flying training with small-scale raids on airfields in Belgium and Holland where German bombers were known to be massing.

Flying, whether in combat or while training, was not without its dangers, even in front-line squadrons that had the pick of the latest aircraft to roll off the production lines. But there were dangers too on the ground. This was illustrated in a shocking incident that occurred on 27 July. As Battle L5528 was being prepared for that night's operation, a bomb fell from its racks and started to burn. Those inside the aircraft leapt out and heroically started to beat the flames, where they were joined in their endeavours by members of the groundcrew and headquarters staff. Their efforts, however, were in vain, and moments later a terrific explosion ripped through the aircraft and the men standing around, leaving them no chance of escape. Ten men were killed outright and the eleventh died the next day. Among the dead were the aircraft's skipper, Walter Blom, a Tasmanian who had earned the Distinguished Flying Cross in France for an incident in which he had returned from pressing home an attack on a motorised column with his aircraft badly damaged and his own flying suit drenched in aviation fuel. The citation made mention of his outstanding courage and tenacity in bringing the crippled bomber home. It was ironic that after surviving such a baptism of fire, he was to be killed in an accident in the comparative safety of the UK. Three days later the funerals of two of the deceased took place at nearby East Bridgeford parish church and at the request of the relatives the bodies of the others were sent to their homes where separate funerals took place the following day.

Despite the trauma, everyday life continued, both on the squadron and at home. RAF Newton was a pre-war airfield built in 1937, and when not on duty Eric scoured the local area for digs for Betty so that she could be close by. Leave was very scarce, but he was determined to spend what little time he had with his wife.

By the middle of August 1940, Britain was in a fight for its life in a battle that bore its name. The Germans were determined to invade and had a plan, Operation Sealion, agreed and ready to go and started moving men and material to the ports of northern France in preparation for the attack. They also began assembling a huge armada of barges and other vessels required to make the short hop across the Channel. But for any land campaign to succeed, the attacker first needs to have air supremacy, and to this end the pilots of the Royal Air Force were being particularly obstinate and obstructive. Actually they were winning, and when the commander of the Luftwaffe, Hermann Göring and his generals shifted the focus away from attacking RAF airfields to concentrate on blitzing British cities, they lost any potential advantages they had earlier gained. The leaders had been misled by the exaggerated claims of their own pilots and believed that Fighter Command was down to its last 100 fighters[16]; they also believed that a few more daylight raids on London might complete the ruin of the city's defences. They were wrong on both counts, but while the threat of invasion remained, it was up to the RAF's bomber aircraft to do everything they could to take the fight to the Germans. As Winston Churchill so famously said in his speech citing the bravery of 'The Few', the fighters might be the country's salvation, but the bombers alone provided the means of victory.

Throughout the month the squadron trained, liaising with army units in simulated low-level dive-bombing attacks and sweeps of the North Sea to hunt imaginary troop ships and U-boats, encouraged by the support of their new AOC No. 1 Group, John Breen. They also lost some of their number to fighter squadrons, the need for trained pilots to fly Spitfires and Hurricanes of even greater urgency to the national war effort. Among those who volunteered, Peter Crofts, was shot down and killed within days of arriving at No. 605 Squadron via No. 615 at Prestwick. He managed to bail out having come out second best to a dogfight with Bf109s but fell to his death. Another, Spencer Peacock-Edwards, survived the battle to achieve success in Malta and finish the war as an 'ace'. A third, George Stroud, was shot down in flames, becoming one of Sir Archibald McIndoe's famous 'Guinea Pigs', the nickname given to those operated on by the Scottish surgeon and pioneer in the treatment of burns. It was to one of McIndoe's disciples, that Eric would later owe a significant debt of gratitude.

A handful of new aircrew arrived on the squadron during that period, among them a well-travelled and experienced future squadron commander, Robert Carter. Carter was a former Halton Apprentice (16th Entry), one of the famed 'Trenchard Brats' who did such sterling work throughout the war and subsequently. Trained as a Fitter, and a contemporary of the Olympic hurdler Don Finlay to whom he always finished second best, Robert was marked out for stardom early and awarded a cadetship to Cranwell and learned how to fly. Upon qualifying he was posted to No. 27 Squadron the Northwest Frontier, dropping leaflets from a Westland Wapiti biplane to warn warring factions to cease their activities or face the bombing of their villages. He progressed his early operational career with No. 11 Squadron, continuing to patrol the troublesome region, before returning to the UK in 1936 to command, rather imaginatively, a pilotless aircraft flight (effectively converted Tiger Moths known as 'Queen Bees') engaged in anti-aircraft co-operation. He was posted to No. 150 Squadron as a flight commander on 5 August. It was to Carter that went the honour of leading the squadron's first concerted offensive drive since its return from France.[17]

On 7 September 1940, London was blitzed by German bombers in a devastating attack and the following day all squadron personnel were recalled from leave immediately, believing an invasion to be imminent. It was the start of a few weeks of intense operational activity, as the Battles were increasingly pressed into service to conduct nighttime raids on shipping and invasion barges now gathered in the ports of Calais and Boulogne. Carter led attacks on the night of 7th and 9th, but Eric had to wait until 11th before his name and that of his observer, Sergeant Armstrong and wireless operator, Sergeant Leigh (Hillyard's replacement), appeared on the Battle Order of three crews required for operations that night.

A significant weight of bombs was loaded: to a now standard cluster of 16 x 40-pound GP bombs housed inside the bomb-bay were added an 'overload' of two 250-pound bombs, one beneath each wing. It took the total bomb load to 1,140-pounds, exceeding its design limits.

In the event it proved something of an anti-climax. Carter, who was meant to be the first to get away, never left the ground, after suffering hydraulic issues with his brakes. Eric took off but returned having run into bad weather which reduced visibility to virtually zero. Only one of the three, Victor Spiller, enjoyed any success, but even he experienced problems when he was momentarily blinded by liquid spraying out from behind the hydraulic press gauge, obliging him to switch off his engine and glide. It was an anxious time for the young pilot before he was able to re-start the engine and continue for home.[18]

Eric had better luck on 17th, when he was again detailed to accompany Carter and a third Battle, flown by 'Tiny' Elliott for an attack on a concentration of barges in Boulogne. Elliott was the first away and upon reaching the target made a successful gliding attack, releasing a stick of bombs from 7,000ft and having the satisfaction of seeing them explode across the outer basin of the harbour. Carter took off a little later, and on arriving over Boulogne found the weather conditions so poor that he made for Calais as an alternative target. He dropped his 250-pound bombs from height, one exploding on the mole, before mounting a dive-bombing attack and coming down to 2,000ft to release his smaller 40-pounders. Almost instantly his aircraft was subjected to an intense barrage of anti-aircraft fire, flak shells bursting dangerously close as he jinked and weaved away from the target and made good his escape.[19]

The last of the trio to make their attack was Battle L5548 with Eric at the controls. He was able to see Boulogne and release his bombs on the target, the crew all agreeing that they had seen a good 'stick' bursting across the harbour. He was troubled neither by flak nor searchlights and landed back at base after a trip of less than three hours, fully satisfied with his night's work.

The task was repeated on 22nd, Eric enjoying probably his most successful attack to date. This time the raid was scheduled for the small hours of the morning, and instead of a large number of smaller GP bombs, the armourers had gone for four 250-pounders. Eric, with his usual crew, had no trouble in identifying the target or dropping his bombs which exploded along the quayside, causing a substantial fire. A small amount of light flak was encountered but it didn't trouble them, and Eric landed home just as dawn was breaking.

After a month of frenetic activity at the base, the squadron received a visit from the Secretary of State for Air, Sir Archibald Sinclair who spoke to the pilots and praised them for their part in keeping the enemy at bay.

They perhaps knew little of the results they had achieved; operational pilots rarely had visibility of campaign success, only the success or otherwise of their own raids. They might form an opinion based on their squadron efforts, and to this end No. 150 Squadron had performed well, and suffered no casualties, which was a blessed relief after the debacle in France.

When the facts were known, the bombers had done much profitable work.[20] By the middle of September, German preparations for an invasion had reached their peak. On 15th, Intelligence sources suggested there were 102 barges in Boulogne; two days later this figure peaked at 150. By the same date the 136 barges in Calais on 13 September had increased to 266. By 18 September, the Channel ports held more than 1,000 barges and a further 600 waited up-river at Antwerp. Through the efforts of the Battles of No. 150 Squadron, however, and those of the Blenheim, Wellington, Whitley and Hampden squadrons who now had no trouble in finding their targets and could carry a maximum bombload thanks to the shorter distances involved, German invasion plans were thwarted. Twelve percent of the invasion force was destroyed, and considerable damage inflicted on the port and harbour infrastructure which hampered the Germans in their task of organisation, minesweeping and assembly. Invasion plans were postponed and eventually cancelled.

By 23 September, photographic reconnaissance suggested there were signs that an immediate crisis had been averted. Several German destroyers which had been present were no longer there, and the number of barges in the ports between Flushing and Boulogne had decreased by nearly a third.

Chapter Three

Saying Boo to an Alligator

At the beginning of October, the squadron was effectively stood down to allow conversion to a new type of aircraft, the Vickers Wellington. Whereas the Fairey Battle had been a huge disappointment, the Wellington was an altogether different proposition. Designed to Air Ministry specification B9/32 of September 1932, the prototype 'Wimpey', as it was affectionately known, flew on 15 June 1936, and its sleek lines attracted a great deal of attention at the RAF Display at Hendon when she was seen in public for the first time. The first production Wellington made its initial flight at the end of 1937, and while it differed considerably from the prototype (the fuselage and tail were redesigned, and gun turrets fitted) it still comprised the same geodetic[21] lattice-work construction that made it immensely strong and which many crews would have cause to thank for the damage she could sustain and still fly. Two Bristol Pegasus engines, one on each wing, gave her a top speed of 235mph at 15,500ft and the first Wellingtons to reach a frontline squadron could carry 4,500-pounds of bombs 1,200 miles, or double the range with a quarter of the bombload.

Like the Fairey Battle squadrons, the first Wellington crews had had a tough time of their early engagement with the enemy. An official belief that a unit of Wellingtons, flying in formation, was more than enough to ward off German fighters in daylight was soon exposed for the folly that it was.

Converting from one type of aircraft to another in the winter of 1940 was a somewhat haphazard affair, especially since aircraft were in short supply. Some of the pilots had already been detached to another squadron (No. 214 Squadron at Stradishall) to learn to fly the Wellington and then became 'instructors' to the rest of the squadron's pilots having mastered their craft. It would be some time before the more co-ordinated infrastructure of Conversion Units (CUs), Heavy Conversion Units (HCUs) and Finishing Schools would be established to streamline the process.

On the afternoon of 2 October, the squadron heard the sound of an unfamiliar engine overhead, and soon after, witnessed the landing of the first Wellington to arrive at Newton. A second arrived the following day and within a week the squadron had an establishment of ten aircraft, allowing conversion training to begin in earnest both at Newton and neighbouring Stradishall. It was not long, however, before tragedy struck. On 11 October, Charles Rafter, a 22-year-old flying officer who had been one of the first to fly the Wellington, set out from Stradishall in the late afternoon for a training flight. As the Wellington sped along the runway, it began to swing alarmingly to starboard at which point the pilot lost control and the aircraft crashed into the corner of a large hangar and burst into flames. Both pilot and co-pilot were killed along with two other members of the crew. Two more were seriously injured.

The accident did not stop the training. If anything, it served to increase its intensity. Being winter, the weather often got in the way, with heavy showers and constant rain, but when conditions were favourable enough, the squadron took every opportunity to fly. Air firing practices, cross-countries and navigation exercises were frequent, although some had to be abandoned part-way through as the clouds started to build.

Back in Teddington Betty's sister Claudia was making preparations for her wedding to Alf Lock. It was to take place on 15 November at the church where Eric and Betty had got married less than a year earlier and they were both excitedly looking forward to it, providing Eric could get the necessary leave. With the squadron's conversion fast coming to an end, Eric knew it was only a matter of time before they would once again be declared 'operational'. Five days before the wedding, on the 10th, Eric wrote to Alf:

> The 'operations' snag is still the only bug-bear as regards my leave, but I think 10-to-1 it'll be ok.

Three days after writing the letter, on the evening of 13 November, Eric was detailed for a local night dual instruction flight, as second pilot to Paul Carlyon, a 28-year-old Canadian pilot officer serving in the RAF (as opposed to the Royal Canadian Air Force, RCAF) who had only been on the squadron a few weeks but already had some experience on Wellingtons.

Allocated Wellington N2998, a Mk1a (it could be distinguished from the Mk1 in that it had different manufacturers' gun turrets, Nash and Thompson as opposed to Vickers), they took off shortly after 1930 hours, but within less than half an hour the visibility deteriorated to such as degree that Carlyon decided to cut short the instruction and sought permission to land. In the meantime, a Wellington from No. 103 Squadron, with whom 150 shared a base, had crash-landed before them, coming to rest on the left

-hand side of the flare path. Whether the pilot had made a mess of the landing is a moot point, but as the bomber touched down it swung out of control and veered off the runway before coming to rest. All six crew, including the sergeant pilot Charles Muggeridge, managed to make it out safely, shaken but unhurt[22]. Little more than a wreck and presenting something of a dangerous obstacle, the ground crews were quickly out to mark the damaged aircraft with lights as a warning to others. A second aircraft, a Hampden from RAF Cottesmore, also landed without incident.

Because of the increasing gloom, a decision was taken not to turn on the floodlight to guide the aircraft in, since it would likely hinder rather than help their approach. The electrical flare path was at full brilliance and supplemented by 'gooseneck flares', a wick-in-kerosene arrangement that looked like small watering cans. Carlyon switched on the aircraft landing light and brought the Wellington in at an angle of 45-degrees from the central line of the flare path, dissecting the third and fourth flare that marked the runway. As the wheels touched the ground Carlyon and Eric at last caught sight of the stranded Wellington but too late to avoid a collision. With tragic inevitability and with the sickening sound of metal upon metal, the No. 150 Squadron Wellington collided with the wrecked No. 103 Squadron aircraft and both machines immediately burst into flames.

Unbuckling his harness and scrambling from his seat, Carlyon made it out of the burning Wellington in double quick time, fully expecting to see his co-pilot directly behind him. When it became clear that Eric hadn't followed, Carlyon, despite his own injuries, bravely returned to the cockpit to find Eric struggling frantically with his parachute harness that had somehow become snagged, pinning him to his seat. Being a particularly tall man, Carlyon was able to reach around and release Eric's harness, such that both men could scramble clear. Only just in time, for now their Wellington was well-ablaze and the heat intense. The 'blood wagon'[23] arrived to take Eric to the sick bay, but after a brief examination of his injuries, Eric was transferred to Nottingham City hospital. He not only had some nasty third-degree burns to his hands but a badly hurt right knee that the medical authorities warned might never truly heal. It would almost certainly cause him some disability in later life.

Eric had been lucky; Paul Carlyon had undoubtedly saved his life, and his commendable action recorded in the squadron ORB. Others had been decorated for less with the George Medal, but Carlyon had to content himself with the satisfaction that he had done Eric a good turn.[24]

Eric's admission to hospital and the severity of his injuries meant he was unable to attend Claudia and Alf's wedding but he was sufficiently well for him and Betty to send a telegram, wishing them every future happiness.

While he was being treated, investigators into the crash took statements from the pilot:

> Coming into land I had difficulty lining up with the flare path. I was unable to line up with it perfectly and after landing ran through the flare path at an angle. Immediately after running through the flare path, I hit another crashed machine which I had not seen, nor had I been able to see the red lights around it.

The engineering officer confirmed that the aircraft was completely burned out but also what, if anything, was salvageable from the wreck: 'Port engine intact but probably subjected to considerable heat. Starboard engine wrenched off and damaged but not subjected to great heat. Mid turret slightly damaged only. Rear turret burned out. Front turret considerably damaged.' The unit commander concluded that the incident had occurred due to a 'misjudged approach during night landing'. No further action was taken.[25]

Eric remained in hospital for the next five weeks and on 3 December he and Betty celebrated their first wedding anniversary from Eric's hospital bed. Two days later Betty wrote to Claudia (usually known as Claud or Clu) and new husband Alf, thanking them for their anniversary card and describing the occasion:

> We had quite a little celebration at the hospital. I took roses and chrysanths, a big box of chocs, grapes and Turkish delight, and a good strong stick for when he starts to hobble about. He wanted that very much, because it won't be long now. I also took a chocolate cake and stuck one candle on it (he! he!) and one of the Polish officers in there brought in a bottle of sherry and he and his friends toasted us. It was quite fun, one of the nurses wanted to know if it was Eric's birthday with the cards and flowers etc. We had a few visitors from the 'drome too, so in all, we had a very pleasant afternoon and evening.

She went on to write:

> Oh I forgot to tell you that Eric bought me a present too! It was a pleasant surprise. I didn't dream of getting anything, but apparently he'd asked the nurse to get it for him. It was a box of pretty hand-embroidered hankies and a gold lacy afternoon tablecloth. I don't really need the latter, but he wasn't well enough to think of much else and he knows I like them. I was especially pleased because he'd written me a

little note all by himself, it wasn't half quavery! He is improving, by leaps and bounds, quite different to when you saw him. Did I tell you that we hoped to go home for Christmas after all? We are looking forward to it (apart from the bombs). Mam says they had it terribly last Friday. I suppose you have heard all about it. Poor old Fred Cross and our poor old car, to say nothing of the garage* being hit! I can hardly believe it, I wonder what Dad'll do now! This B------ war!!'

*(Betty's father owned a small petrol station, always known as the garage.)

On 16 December Eric was transferred to RAF Hospital Rauceby, the site of a former lunatic asylum. Rauceby had been taken over by the RAF a few months before Eric was admitted. The rapid expansion of the RAF throughout Lincolnshire had meant the established RAF hospital at Cranwell was no longer sufficient to cope with the number of casualties coming through its doors. A new site at Nocton Hall was acquired, but even before it was opened it was considered too small and so No. 4 RAF Hospital at Rauceby was born.

Now in the care of a dedicated Crash and Burns Unit in the very capable hands of Fenton Braithwaite, the resident plastic surgeon, Eric's recovery accelerated. He was given a week's Special Leave to be with his family following the death of his father and was readmitted to Rauceby the day after Boxing Day for further treatment until at last, in the first week of the New Year of 1941, was transferred to RAF Hospital Torquay to convalesce for the next ten weeks. Just before this transfer, and still in some discomfort, he wrote in a very shaky hand to Claud and Alf:

Yes, this is written by the great bandaged hand you saw on your visit. Now, I'm almost the old Eric A. B. you always knew.

During his long convalescence in Torquay, he and Betty were able to spend some time together away from the war. They enjoyed many days out, including a visit to Primley Zoo, Paignton, which Eric described humorously and in some detail in a letter written to Claud and Alf on 5 February:

I must record that with the usual daring of a Pilot Officer in His Majesty's Royal Air Force, I summoned up sufficient courage to say 'boo' to an alligator, but the obstinate thing didn't bat an eyelid.

With further intrepidity, we advanced upon a free, liberated peacock (rude name, I always think) in a fruitless attempt to borrow one of its feathers for Bet's hat. It was a proud, stuck-up, snobbish peacock, anyway – obviously public school. From the peacock we went into and straight out of the rabbit house; not that I dislike the sweet little animals in the least, but they do smell.

The biggest attraction, I shrink to admit, was the children's playground. Betty simply could not hold herself from the helter-skelter – such a dangerous amusement I think – and I was forced to stand by at the terminus, while she, skirts etc. flying, came hurtling down the slipway; terribly brave girl, you know. Then, while she took further chances on the see-saw-swing, I was fully employed in keeping in motion the push-me-round revolving platform for the benefit of the kiddies (not ours, of course).

We finished the day by making pigs of ourselves – not literally, of course – in the café.

The letter continues in a more serious tone, with a hint of the challenges ahead:

Getting all serious, I must thank you for your good wishes as regards my health and must point out that I am getting on too well. I shall, eventually, but not yet awhile I hope, be going back to Nottingham. The knee is now bent sufficiently to prevent a limp in my walk, but not quite enough for flying (sigh of relief).

One of the places they visited while in Devon was the little village of Cockington, not far from Torquay, where they enjoyed a relaxing few days, taking photos of one another and of the surrounding area. But the idyll didn't last.

On Eric's discharge from hospital on 18 March, a full four months after his near-fatal accident, he reported to the Central Medical Establishment at RAF Halton in Buckinghamshire for a medical assessment and was found fit to return to his unit. The road to recovery had been a long haul but not without its pleasures.

A few days after his return to duty Eric was posted to the No 2 Air Navigation School at RAF Cranage in Cheshire for a short navigator instructor's course.

While at Cranage, Eric wrote a poem to Betty for her twenty-third birthday, describing her impulsive spontaneity. He called her Bet, as did her parents and siblings, and signed it with the name 'John', which was the special name they both privately used for him, ending with the usual seven kisses.

On Your Birthday, 1941.

Dear Bet,

If it wasn't for your cheek
And the saucy way you speak:
(How you flagrantly declare,
'That you really do not care')

If you didn't thrill right through,
When a baby smiles at you.

If you didn't jump and dance
And get excited, when, perchance,
I take you out to buy a dress;
(These things bring me such happiness)

If you said, just 'Hullo John',
When I'd been a long time gone.

If it wasn't for your smile,
When I'm sad a little while,
And your tenderness and care,
When I'm worried – in despair.

If it wasn't for your eyes,
Like the stars up in the skies,
Each one shining, sparkling, gleaming –
Darkened only when you're sleeping.

If it wasn't for your joy
At little things – like 'girl meets boy'.

If it wasn't for the bliss,
When I hold you in a kiss:
(Whom, but we, could ever capture
Such supreme and perfect rapture!)

If it wasn't for your kindness,
Helping me in all my blindness,
Soothing me in all my ills –
(Far more help than doctors' pills).

If it wasn't for your love, ----
And for God's blessing from above -----
I'd divorce you!

Yours ever,
John

Having successfully completed his course, Eric was posted in the middle of May for staff navigation duties with No 3 Air Observers Navigation School (3 AONS) at Bobbington, Staffordshire, which comprised a contingent of forty officers and thirty-five aircraft.[26] Under the command of Thomas Q Horner (soon to be promoted group captain), 3 AONS was a small cog in an otherwise massive training wheel for new aircrew destined for Bomber Command.[27]

Just a few weeks prior to Eric's arrival, the unit's previous CO, Raymond Pakenham, a former army officer, had taken delivery of the first Botha, a hugely unpopular and disappointing twin-engine aircraft from the Blackburn Aircraft Company. The Botha had originally been designed as a torpedo bomber for Coastal Command and by every measure was a failure, so much so that it had been relegated to an operational training role within six months of it entering operational service, and two years later had been declared obsolete!

Poor reliability meant the Bothas were regularly unserviceable[28], and training was also at the mercy of the weather. It meant it was not until 7 June that Eric started flying in earnest and was happy when Betty moved to Staffordshire to be near him. They found rooms to rent at Enville, not far from Stourbridge, from Reverend and Mrs Fisher. The vicar and his wife became good friends, and they spent plenty of time together at the old rectory as well as their nearby flat.

On 28 June Brian Baker, the AOC No. 51 Group and a first world war fighter pilot[29] arrived on the station with John Whitford, a group captain[30], to help re-organise the flying schedule to make up for lost time. Too few aircraft and pilots to fly them was hampering progress and reducing the flying hours available to each pupil. Both pilots and aircraft became even fewer two days later when a Botha crashed nearby. Suffering an engine failure on take-off it stalled and crashed at Halfpenny Green. The pilot, Peter Purdon, and trainee observers Leading Aircraftmen Albert Chester and Derek Amos were killed. Betty and Eric were keenly aware of this tragedy happening so close; the horrors of war were never far away, and Eric felt a sense of responsibility as one of the more senior instructors.

Promoted to the acting rank of flight lieutenant on 17 July, Eric's days were filled with bringing new recruits up to speed with both basic and more advanced navigation techniques, flying not only Bothas but also Ansons which steadily replaced its disappointing stablemate. He also took his turn as a 'chaser', an officer whose duty was to check the hours flown, hours on the ground, and reasons for 'non-flying' of every aircraft, analysing the results to further improve operational efficiency.

With Betty so close, they spent every spare moment they could together, and with friends, including new ones Eric was making on the station. Betty describes that period in a letter to Claud and Alf at the end of August 1941:

> I've been meeting quite a few of Eric's pals lately. Johnny Good fetched me the other night when Eric was working late and we had some drinks at the mess while waiting for Eric, then we all went to the Hippodrome. He's only got a two-seater so I was squeezed between the two of them! We did have some fun – I was introduced to a Pims!! Ever tried them? I quite liked them and had two, not realising they were very intoxicating (on an empty tummy too, and I'd already had a gin and lime!) Of course Eric and Johnny egged me on and the consequence was……. I went home singing at the top of my voice and when I got out of the car I positively tottered! Eric and Johnny were tickled to death – I didn't mind, I thoroughly enjoyed myself, it was a perfect scream. Nice bloke Johnny, he's just become a father and is very proud of himself.[31]
>
> Last night Eric brought home two other chaps (or rather they brought him, in their car) and we all went to the Lido. They came back to supper afterwards, luckily I had just about enough, it was salad and sardines. They thoroughly enjoyed it anyway and said it was a damn sight better than the mess. We had quite a pleasant evening. They were nice blokes too, very funny and all that.
>
> It'll be nice to be on our own tonight! I don't want them to make a habit of coming, good fun though they are – rations just won't run to it! It's the Royal Engineers (REs) that are billeted here, I think they're going to tidy up the place - roads and things. It would be nice if they were the Pay Corps and Alf was transferred. I'd like you to see Enville. You must pop up here some time, I should love you to see our little flat.

At the start of the New Year of 1942, Eric was given additional training, both at RAF Bridgnorth and at Stanmore, where he attended a short course on new R/T procedures. He returned to find the school in 'a constant battle against the weather', Eric being pictured in the snow near Enville. The only positive spin on the negative weather was that it gave Eric time to enjoy one of his favourite pastimes, ice skating.

By now the training unit had almost doubled in size and had more than forty Ansons on strength. It had also been divided into four Flights: an Armament Flight, two day navigation Flights and a night navigation Flight.

In April 1942 Claud and Alf went to visit and Eric was pleased to see them, for the strain of many hours of flying (Eric could sometimes be flying more than nine hours a day) was draining him mentally and physically, so much so that he developed lumbago. Of greater concern to many of his fellow instructors, and especially those who proudly wore the 'Flying Arsehole', was that their observer's categorisation would be no more, and their 'trade' split between 'navigators' and 'air bombers'. It was not a surprise. The increasing sophistication of the bomber aircraft, and a better understanding of practical issues facing bomber crews, made it obvious that the roles of navigating and bomb aiming were too much for one man. It led to the creation of the 'PNB' (Pilot, Navigator and Bomb Aimer) scheme for future training, all three being given some responsibility for navigation but every man also given an allotted task. Some of the old sweats steadfastly refused to call themselves anything but observers for the rest of the war, and an apparent shortage of navigators' brevets meant that some navigators and bomb aimers received the observers' brevet, even as late as 1944, adding to the confusion. The No. 3 AONS records capture the mood of the time in an entry from 11 May regarding the first official information regarding the trade of air bomber: 'A trade not received with any enthusiasm by many u/t air observers with few exceptions. All air observers at the school have come to the conclusion that they are expert navigators and not so good bombers!'

Eric recovered from his lumbago after being prescribed a short course of treatment, and he was soon back on his feet and in a more positive state of mind. On 30 May he wrote, 'I am now, once more, the bright and happy soul you know me always to be.'

The date was a propitious one. That night, Sir Arthur Harris, who had only recently taken over as the Commander-in-Chief of Bomber Command, mounted the first of his showpiece 'Thousand Bomber Raids' on the city of Cologne. Operation Millennium, as it was called, comprised 1,047 aircraft in all, the figure achieved not only by using every aircraft in Bomber Command, but also scraping together a rag-tag bunch of aircraft and scratch crews from Coastal and Training Command to reach the magic number and give Harris his PR victory.

The ambition had been well trailed. Harris had given orders some weeks in advance that the men under his command, including those in the training groups, were to make men available 'on special attachment' to operational units by the end of the month.

Eric was perhaps fortunate not to be flying, since more than forty aircraft failed to return that night – a good proportion of those from OTUs and other training establishments. Among the aircrew missing was one of his fellow officers, Hector Batten. He'd grabbed the chance to navigate a Wellington from Feltwell belonging to the Central Gunnery School at Sutton Bridge, only to be shot down by a German nightfighter. Batten, along with the pilot and three other members of the crew were killed; one bailed out and spent the rest of the war as a prisoner.[32]

Eric spent eighteen months at No. 3 AONS, during which time the make-up of the school changed significantly. Not unusually for the time, especially for a training establishment, the station comprised both service and civilian personnel, and there was much rejoicing when civilian contractors from Marshalls of Cambridge vacated their huts 'to the great satisfaction of the service personnel on the station'. As one of the more senior officers, Eric had other duties to fulfil besides flying. On 9 July he presided over a Court of Inquiry near Crewe into a collision between an RAF Staff car, a civilian motor cyclist and a Leading Aircraftman (LAC) in which the motor cyclist had received fatal injuries. He took this responsibility in his stride and carried it out with great efficiency.

On the same day another enquiry was held into the loss of one of the school's Avro Ansons over the Isle of Man. The Anson (L7927) had taken off at 11.00hrs on the morning of 26 June on a navigation training exercise when it was seen flying very low and very slow over the capital city, Douglas. Witnesses described seeing bits falling from the aircraft and then a loud 'pop', whereupon the port wing appeared to crumple, causing the Anson to turn and dive into the ground. All the crew were killed. Two days later another Anson flew low over the crash site to take photographs that would be shown to the subsequent Inquiry.[33]

That summer Eric's mother went to visit her son and daughter-in-law at their flat in Enville. Eric mentioned this in a letter to Claud and Alf on 11 July:

> My mother had a good time up here and we are very much looking forward to the arrival of the Barrys. They are due on the 19th now, as Des is at home unexpectedly next week. They are coming by train of course, because of the new petrol control. I wish I could get away to see Des, but of course the Station would collapse without me!

On 31 July there were general complaints about hygiene on the Station. The kitchens were completely inadequate, there were numerous complaints about the food, many officers were sick, and a sewage farm was tested for water pollution. Three weeks later Eric succumbed and returned home for 24 hours to recover.

It was not until the middle of October 1942, that Eric's 'rest' at air observers' school finally came to an end, by which time he had added several hundred more hours of flying into his logbook. Harris was intent on increasing the strength of Bomber Command after a brief period in which it looked like he might lose most of his squadrons to Coastal Command (to fight in the Battle of the Atlantic). The unquestionably tough C-in-C managed to ride out the storm and face down any opposition, thanks in no small way to the continued support of the Prime Minister, Winston Churchill. Harris' expansion plans, however, needed experienced airmen and crews, and so on 13 October, Eric said his goodbyes and thank you's to his colleagues and the Reverend and Mrs Fisher with a posting to No. 29 OTU at RAF North Luffenham. Betty, in the meantime, moved back to 23 Mays Road and began working at the National Physical Laboratory (N.P.L) in Teddington. This was where Barnes Wallis tested and developed his famous 'bouncing bombs' to be used in the Dambusters' raid the following spring, although Betty's work was of a more humble nature.

Eric was, of course, familiar with the concept of operational training, but the OTUs of 1942/43 were on a significantly larger scale than the ones he had been used to prior to his posting to France almost three years earlier. Bomber Command was fast-becoming 'industrialised' in the way it was manufacturing and producing new crews to feed the increasing number of four-engine bomber aircraft now equipping the frontline squadrons. In Bomber Command's Order of Battle for April 1942 there were only fourteen squadrons equipped with four-engine aircraft – a mix of Short Stirlings, Handley Page Halifaxes, and Avro Lancasters. One squadron (No. 150 Squadron at RAF Snaith) also had a small number of Consolidated Liberators on trial. The rest were primarily equipped with Wellingtons, Manchesters (the forerunner to the Lancaster but with two rather than four engines), and the odd Hampden. By April 1943, the Hampdens had all-but disappeared and only a handful of Wellington squadrons remained. The three principal four-engine bombers dominated.

RAF North Luffenham was a new station in the heart of Rutland, perched on high ground close to the Georgian splendour of Stamford. For a time, it had been home to the Hampdens and Manchesters of No. 61 Squadron, a squadron with which Eric would soon become familiar, but for now it was a training establishment under the command of Rudolph 'Taffy' Taaffe. Taaffe, an Irishman, was a no-nonsense pre-war regular who had served in Kenya and Iraq, and who for a time was chosen as personal assistant to Robert Brooke-Popham, the man unfairly blamed for allowing the fall of Singapore to the Japanese.

Alumni at the OTU included Les Munro, the New Zealander who

achieved fame with No. 617 Squadron later in the war. He survived a crash towards the end of his training, and just a few weeks prior to Eric's arrival, when his Wellington lost power shortly after take-off, luckily escaping injury. Another who survived an unfortunate accident and was still at North Luffenham for the first few weeks of Eric's training, was the Chief Instructor, Freddie Rainsford. 'Turkey' Rainsford, who was 'resting' after an arduous tour in North Africa with No. 148 Squadron, had agreed to teach the commander of the Maintenance Wing how to fly a Wellington. In demonstrating how to land, and concentrating hard, Rainsford forgot to lower his undercarriage, and only realised his error when he heard a crunching sound underneath the aircraft and a fire tender pulling up alongside. Happily for Rainsford, his station commander was understanding, and a 'red' entry into his logbook for such a serious misdemeanour was avoided.[34]

Eric was quickly immersed into the training programme of both ground and flying instruction, dividing his time between North Luffenham and RAF Bruntingthorpe, which later became No. 29 OTU's permanent base. A typical routine of cross-countries, high- and low-level bombing, and combat manoeuvres in the air were complemented by technical and tactical lectures on the ground.

Accidents, injuries and deaths were commonplace at most training units, the inexperience of the crews and the questionable quality of the aircraft, many of which were war-weary veterans well-past their best, were usually to blame. A freak accident on 16 November, however, while Eric was on leave, disproved the general rule. A Wellington with an Australian at the controls was just accelerating down the runway for take-off when it struck fair and square a fuel bowser whose driver had misread a signal and inadvertently pulled out in front of them. By some miracle, no-one was killed, but five of the crew were injured.

Just before their third wedding anniversary, and while Eric was still away, he and Betty learned the joyous news that they were expecting their first child. He returned to the station at the end of the month and not long after his arrival he received a tiny package from his wife containing a small copy of 'Christmas Books' by Charles Dickens containing some of his most famous works. Using the special name Betty had for him, she inscribed the book with the words, 'To my darling John on our 3rd anniversary, with all my love. 3 Dec 1942.'

Eric wrote to Claud and Alf from North Luffenham the same afternoon, having spent several days at Bruntingthorpe, a satellite to North Luffenham that had only just officially opened and was still in chaos. He was very pleased to be back:

I have been back here a little over a week, rather thankfully, as the other place was not fit for civilised people, such as myself, to live in. Truthfully though, it was not too bad over there. It was a change and when the weather was duff for flying we paddled off to the local. The place was in a state of semi-construction and we had to slosh through mud everywhere. It was completely in the wilds and the only other attraction apart from the locals, was Leicester[35], which we could only get to once a week on the service bus, for an evening's fun and games. I did manage to get home one night, being back the next evening, but it was a very difficult business getting back. I fear I shall be going back there (Bruntingthorpe, not home) in a week or two for a further short period.

Referencing Bet's work at the Laboratory, Eric added:

As you probably know now, Bet is enjoying herself playing about with decimals and thousandths parts of an inch (in a vice) at the N.P.L. It is very tiring for her and in fact she cannot tighten or untighten the vice. I've told her to pack it in if she can't 'stand it'. Standing up all the while 'gets her down', as you must know.

Later that month, as soon as the pregnancy was confirmed, Eric wrote a poem in the form of a sonnet to his unborn child, dated 15 December 1942.

> Let us Prepare.
> Beyond the far horizon, slowly, creeps
> A new beginning of a life to be,
> So let us, while the unborn baby sleeps,
> Prepare a path in God; - and let us see
> That all its infant fears and childish woes
> Are banished from its troubled mind; our eye -
> Our parent eye - must watch and check these foes
> In youth and never let our baby cry
> For want of love and guidance or a kind
> And understanding friend; - for out of love
> And kindness grows a stronger will, a mind
> More resolute to face, with God above,
> The daily trials of this life on earth.
> Prepare us, now, O God, for this new birth.

Eric was longing to get home again, even more so now with his impending fatherhood. He was desperate for more leave, even if only a short, forty-eight-hour pass, and determined to increase his flying hours on which the leave rota was based. He wrote, 'I've done quite a lot of flying and want to 'plug' it, so that I might get some leave. There is little chance of even a '48' for a long time yet.'

He was also excited by the thought of becoming a parent. His sister already had a child, a daughter Sylvia born earlier that year (he had been invited to the Christening but unable to attend), and he now very much wanted a child of his own. In a further letter to Claud and Alf he said, 'Yes, I like being an uncle, but it would be much more fun to be a daddy.' Happily, Eric was able to be together with his wife before Christmas, and the two spent much of the time discussing possible names. It did not take them long to decide on John for a boy and Jeannie for a girl. Eric returned to North Luffenham on Christmas Day.

As the old year of 1942 faded and the New Year of 1943 was born, Eric was nearing the end of his operational training. Despite his past injuries, and his experiences over France, he still enjoyed the sensation of flying, and treated the whole thing as a bit of fun. Even when he found himself on more than one occasion inadvertently entangled with his country's own defences, he still saw it all as just part of a huge game organised for his own entertainment. One example illustrates the point. On 3 January he wrote to Claud and Alf about finding himself caught in the middle of a Balloon barrage, bags of lighter-than-air gas tethered to the ground by steel cables to deter low-flying aircraft:

> I've been flying for four nights in succession – and some day flying. Last night I did a four and a half hour trip and got mixed up in Balloons everywhere – but not really – they were close-hauled. How did I know I was in them? – Aha! – We get a secret warning! It was a very nice trip – we were completely lost most of the time. It's great fun being lost at night over England. You don't give a damn, because you can land nearly anywhere if you're running short of petrol – and if you're not, you can soon find yourself by all sorts of means. I like staying lost. On two nights we've had to land at the other 'drome, nearer you, and return here next day, as the surface of this 'drome is bad and a bit risky for night landings. I'm glad I'm pushing on with my flying – it brings me nearer some leave at the end of the course – probably not before the beginning of February.

He finished with, 'What fun to be a Daddy!'

Eric talks of his adventures as though there was little real danger and operational training was something of a lark. A few days later, however, one of his contemporaries, Ernest Kelly, went missing on a 'Nickel' sortie, a trip to drop propaganda leaflets over France that had the added benefit of keeping the German defences occupied and away from a Main Force raid. His Wellington was believed to have been shot down by a night fighter. Two weeks later, John Clark, one of the instructors, was also killed when his aircraft dived straight into the ground inverted having been 'coned' by searchlights.[36]

In the first week of February 1943, with his course successfully completed and his logbook dutifully signed by both the Chief Instructor and Officer Commanding, Eric headed for RAF Swinderby, home to No. 1660 Conversion Unit. He was not alone, for now he also had a crew: a navigator, 'Len' Hewitt; an air bomber, Frederick Steed; a wireless operator, Richard Dinsdale; and an air gunner, Maurice Root-Reed. Hewitt, Steed and Dinsdale were all NCOs, (although Len, a former Customs and Excise officer, was soon commissioned). Root-Reed, rather unusually for an air gunner, was an officer, the result, most probably, of being a former public schoolboy. At 29 he was also a little older than his skipper. Like his captain, he was married.

How airmen came to 'crew up' is the stuff of legend. In the very early days, crews were usually allocated on the squadron, and replacements arrived in individual ones and twos to replace men who were killed, injured or tour-expired, rather than a complete 'unit'. As the aircraft became bigger, and training increased significantly in scale, men tended to be posted to squadrons as whole crews, having chosen their crews at OTU. The usual process was to assemble all the pilots, navigators, air bombers and other trades (wireless operators and air gunners) into one of the giant hangars, where they were told to go and sort themselves out. A pilot might find a navigator, and in turn seek an air bomber to join 'their' crew. Men who had trained together and knew one another, tended to stick together. Men too from the same hometown or background might consider that sufficient grounds to trust one another with their lives. It was a wonderfully chaotic system that worked remarkably well. Of course, there were examples where an individual within a crew did not fit as well as first thought, and might be swapped or replaced, sometimes by mutual consent, but not always. Some pilots 'flunked' it, incapable, for example, of making the transition from single-engine to multi-engine aircraft. Some navigators couldn't navigate, at least not under pressure. None of this would be discovered, however, until they began flying with one another, and getting to better understand one another's strengths and weaknesses.

At the Conversion Unit, and now flying four-engine aircraft with more guns and more complicated systems, the crew increased from five to seven. This included a second air gunner, Joseph Frawley, and a comparatively new trade of flight engineer. When the first four-engine bombers entered service, they had two pilots. Later, and for reasons of practical expediency, it was decided to just have one pilot and share the duties that would have fallen on the second pilot to a flight engineer who monitored the aircraft systems, engines performance, fuel consumption, oil temperatures, etc., to free the pilot for the job of flying the aircraft and captaining his crew. From his correspondence, Eric clearly thought his flight engineer, 23-year old Kenneth Stephenson, a local lad, one of the best.

Whereas Conversion Flights attached to squadrons and the later generation of Conversion Units (rebranded 'Heavy Conversion Units' from October 1942 onwards) were initially equipped with the aircraft a crew would fly on operations, it was not always so. Pilots and crews could find themselves flying a Stirling or a Halifax, only to be posted to a Lancaster squadron. At Swinderby, No. 1660 CU was equipped not only with the Halifax, but also twin-engine Avro Manchesters. It also had the odd Lancaster, an aircraft that was still in desperately short supply, especially for training purposes. Indeed, it was for that very reason that for a brief period in the war, there were also dedicated 'Lancaster Finishing Schools', where crews being posted to a Lancaster squadron could be 'finished' in larger numbers with just a few hours in Lancs, the lion's share of the 'conversion' being done on other types.

The unit lost one of its precious Lancasters on 12 February when, for no apparent reason, Lancaster R5676 broke up in flight not long after take-off, killing all eight on board. The aircraft had more than 200 flying hours to its name, having previously served with No. 106 Squadron. Two days later, the unit lost a Manchester, written off after one of its two Vulture engines burst into flames and the pilot was obliged to force land at RAF Waddington.

Notwithstanding the dangers, Eric wrote to Betty on 25 February, his excitement at becoming a four-engine pilot obvious:

Well, my love, I'm with you again to give you the Gen. He! he! ……….. He! he! What glorious weather still! We're having a fairly busy time here, - but I'm glad, because I like to 'get cracking', otherwise I get a little morose.

Well – I'm a four-engine pilot! He! he! I flew a Halifax around the sky this afternoon. It really was a big thrill to look out either side and see a wing with two bloody great engines on it. These aircraft really are the trolleybuses of the air. He! he! I'm like a kid with a new toy!

I must tell you a rude story I heard a long time ago and which was repeated by the C.O. in his address yesterday. As usual, all the pupils were warned about V.D. and not giving way to local women when under the influence of a little drink. Here's the story: A little mouse lived in a field next to a railway line. One day, he was going out to play and was warned by his mother not to go near the railway. Of course, like all naughty little mice, he immediately went up the railway line. He came to a junction and, while trying to make up his mind which way to go, the points closed and cut off the end of his John Thomas. He ran home to mother and with much scolding, she told him to go back and get the end of his J.T. and she would sew it back on. He found the junction points and put his head down between the points to get his J.T. The points closed again and off came his head!

Moral: Don't lose your head over a little bit of dick!

He! he!

In the same letter, Eric makes reference to the two 'additional' members of his crew, the second air gunner and flight engineer:

I now have a family of seven, with myself, to look after. I have another A/G - a sergeant who seems far more intelligent than my other (pilot officer) - A/G! The 7th is a sergeant flight engineer, who is a very intelligent little chap. He is a very important member and I'm very glad to have this chap.

As I have said, I have been very satisfied with this place, so far. There has been very little to complain about. I went to the station cinema last night and saw a film that made me chuckle and chuckle! 'Between us girls'! Had to get up early for an 8.15 parade this morning. This is held weekly.

Now, darling, I think we shall get a day off on Wednesday week and, with luck, I could get away late Tuesday (9th) afternoon. The question is, - shall I come home or you come to Newark? I think I would prefer to come home, but it means I would have to get away in time to get a reasonable train on the Tuesday. Your coming up here would give us much more time together, but (i) I've got to find a hotel with accommodation (ii) it's a tiring journey for you and (iii) it would be miserable for you to have to journey home, afterwards. On the other hand, you could perhaps stay for a few days, as I could probably get off quite early some days – we don't night fly for about three weeks! I think I must make some enquiries about a hotel as soon as I can, eh?

Laundry! – I won't send any, after all, as there is so much and I can't get hold of a box. My batman is a good chap and promised to wash me out a set of underclothes. The rest will be done in about 10 days at the laundry.

Eric's time at the Conversion Unit was relatively short, but pilot and flight engineer had the most to gain from the additional instruction. Pilot and crew were kept fully occupied both in the air and on the ground, for the first week of any new crew's training was given over to ground instruction. Flying training, when it began, was divided into a series of exercises of varying lengths and complexity, designed to test the skills of the individual aircrew categories as well as the performance of the crew as a whole. Exercise one, for example, included dual training on taxying, take-off, climb, and both medium and steep turns. It similarly included three-engine flying, stalling, and a controlled rate of descent to simulate an approach to landing. It lasted two hours and required the close observation of a staff pilot and flight engineer. Exercise 18, the last on which the crews were assessed, involved a five and a half hour 'Bullseye' with the co-operation of fighter and searchlight defences, and the dropping of two bombs on a dedicated range. It was as close to the 'real' thing as the RAF could replicate in a training environment.

Now Eric and the crew were expected to put their new-found skills into practice.

Eric found himself in a constant battle against the weather conditions in the winter of 1942.

Chapter Four

Thundering Through the Clear Air

Happily snatching a few days' leave at home with Betty, Eric reported to No. 61 Squadron on 4 April with the rest of his crew and arrived to find a squadron very much in step with the rhythm of war, a band of brothers with a proud tradition. Originally a fighter squadron formed in the summer of 1917 to defend London from German bombers in the first world war, its nimble single-seater Sopwith Pups and Scouting Experimental (SE) 5s could occasionally be seen snapping at the heels of the mighty multi-engine Gothas above the skies of the capital, but not always able to deliver the killer blow. Disbanded in 1919 along with so many squadrons whose services were no longer required, it was not until the beginning of March 1937 that the squadron was reformed, this time in a bomber capacity, flying Hawker Audax biplanes from RAF Hemswell. Charles Brill arrived to take command a few days later. Originally attached to No. 3 Group, it became part of No. 5 Group in July under the command of William Callaway AFC. Re-equipped with Bristol Blenheims in the New Year of 1938, it converted to Handley Page Hampdens twelve-months later, the type with which it went to war. For its mascot it chose the Lincoln Imp, a famous grotesque on a wall inside Lincoln Cathedral; for its motto: 'Per Purum Tonantes' ('Thundering through the clear air').

Despite its preparedness and constant readiness for war, it was not until Christmas Day of 1939 that it flew its first operational sortie, a sweep of the North Sea by twelve of its aircraft. Claude De Crespigny, who took over command of the squadron from Brill not long after war begun, was to lead the raid with orders to attack any enemy surface vessels in sight. In the event, one of their number returned almost immediately after take-off and while a few vessels were seen, including a submarine, no bombs were dropped. The squadron had to wait till the following spring before making its first bombing attack, one of its aircraft spotting a German destroyer near the Frisian Islands on the night of 7/8 March 1940. Two weeks later they launched their first raid on a German land target, and then in May took part in its first sortie over mainland Germany, just as Eric was preparing to leave for France. They continued night raids over Germany until October the following year.

Avro Manchesters began replacing the Hampdens in the summer of 1941 but teething troubles with the type, in particular its disappointingly unreliable and underpowered Rolls Royce Vulture engines, delayed full equipment for several months. In April 1942, the first Lancasters arrived, and in October the squadron took part in a famous daylight attack on the Schneider factory at Le Creusot. The factory was regarded as the French equivalent of Krupps, producing heavy guns, transport and munitions to support the German military. Harris and the senior commanders and political leaders were acutely aware of the difficulties of attacking a French target employing French workers, and the propaganda victory this would give their enemies if too many French civilians were killed. Harris opted, therefore, to attack in daylight, a hazardous affair at the best of times as an attack six-months earlier over Augsburg had proven, when seven out of twelve Lancasters despatched were shot down. The attack on Le Creusot, situated 300-miles inside France and flown at tree-top level, was rather more successful, and only one of their number was lost. As it happened, this was a No. 61 Squadron aircraft which crashed on the edge of a wood, probably having been hit by flak at low level. The pilot, Squadron Leader W. Duncan Corr DFC and five of his crew were killed. One of the air gunners survived to be taken prisoner. Corr had been the A Flight Commander.

By the spring of 1943, No. 61 Squadron had gained a reputation as a premier Main Force squadron and was very much in the front line of Harris' plans for an assault on the Ruhr that began in March. The Battle of the Ruhr, as it came to be known, and the attack on Germany's industrial might, could not have happened before because Bomber Command simply didn't have the numbers or the technical advantages to conduct what Harris called in his autobiography his 'main offensive'. Now, however, it could regularly call upon 600 bombers or more, the vast majority of them four-engine behemoths, and capable of carrying an even greater weight of bombs. It also had Oboe, an innovative blind bombing device that enabled high-flying, wooden-constructed Mosquitoes from two of the elite RAF Pathfinder squadrons to find and mark targets in the Ruhr with incredible accuracy.

Pathfinders had been formed August 1942 to help find, identify, and mark enemy targets for the Main Force of aircraft to bomb. The arrival of Oboe took the effectiveness of target marking to another level, but the nature of the technology was such that Oboe could not be used beyond the Ruhr. That didn't trouble Harris, not in the short term. He was keen simply to show what his bomber boys were capable of when they had the right tools at their disposal.

Oboe used the Standard Beam Approach (SBA) system of aural indication to guide a pilot along his course. The device was fitted into the aircraft but controlled from ground stations in England. Two stations were involved: the first, known as 'the mouse', directed a radio pulse over the centre of the target. Along this pulse the aircraft travelled, the pilot keeping on track by listening to a continuous note (of an Oboe-like quality, hence the name) which sounded in his earphones. A system of dots and dashes would alert him to any deviation in course. At the same time, the pulse was radiated back by the set within the aircraft, and received by the second ground station, known as 'the cat'. By measuring the time taken for the return pulse to be received, the exact location of the aircraft could be determined, and with incredible accuracy. When the aircraft approached the release point, 'the cat' transmitted the letters 'abcd', then a series of dashes, then a series of dots. As soon as the dots stopped, the bomb aimer pressed his button and the bombs would drop, with an accuracy of the order of 60ft to 200ft.

Eric very quickly settled into squadron life and was at ease with the people around him. In a letter of 10 April, written to Claud, whose husband Alf had been in hospital, he specifically refers to being at 'a nice station with some nice types'. The 'nice station' was RAF Syerston which had been the squadron's home since it moved from RAF Woolfox Lodge almost a year earlier. Syerston, in Nottinghamshire, was a comparatively new airfield built by John Laing & Son and opened in December 1940. For a time, it housed a couple of No. 1 Group Wellington squadrons (Nos 304 and 305 which were both Polish) before being closed while a concrete runway was built along with two colossal T2 hangars. When it re-opened it was re-allocated to No. 5 Group. As well as being home to No. 61 Squadron from May 1942, it was also joined by No. 106 Squadron in the autumn of that same year under the command of Guy Gibson, prior to Gibson's departure to do 'one last trip' to the Dams.

First among the 'nice types' was the hugely popular and widely respected OC, William Penman. Bill Penman, a Scot, had been educated at the Royal High School in Edinburgh, a school with nearly a thousand years of history and recognised as one of the oldest schools in Europe. Its most famous old boy was the author Sir Walter Scott. Among Penman's more direct contemporaries was the world-famous test pilot, Eric 'Winkle' Brown. Penman entered the RAF in 1935 and shared his passion for flying with a passion for sport, turning out for the Scottish Rugby Football XV on several occasions as a full back and captaining the RAF team. Something of an expert flyer and qualifying as a flying instructor, Penman was attached to the RCAF near the beginning of the war, spending more than two years in Canada at a bombing school. His skills were recognised with an Air Force Cross. (AFC). Every inch the man of action, Penman took command of No. 61 Squadron in February 1943, shortly after arriving back in the UK and having been promoted wing commander. He assumed command from Richard Coad AFC. It came as no surprise when he was recommended for the DFC for pressing on to the target on at least two occasions with his gun turrets unserviceable (u/s) or with an engine dead.

Among the other 'nice types' were the flight commanders, Squadron Leaders Rupert Gascoyne-Cecil and Geoffrey Hall. Perhaps somewhat confusingly, whereas a fighter squadron was commanded by a squadron leader, and divided into flights commanded by flight lieutenants, in a bomber squadron it was different. The size and scale of a bomber unit, which included more aircraft (a two-flight squadron would have around 24 aircraft), meant that a squadron was commanded by a wing commander, and squadron leaders put in charge of a flight. At Syerston, Eric was introduced to two of the very best.

Gascoyne-Cecil was typical of the Public School generation of his time. He'd left Stowe, whose alumni included the famed Battle of Britain pilots Tony Bartley, George Barclay, and brothers Hugh and John Dundas, for Balliol where he graduated as a biochemist. While in Oxford, he'd learned to fly with the University Air Squadron and completed his first tour of operations with No. 61 Squadron in the spring of 1942, earning him the first of two DFCs. By the time of Eric's arrival, he was nearing the end of his second tour, around fifty operations in all, and was one of the most experienced airmen on the station.

Geoffrey Hall was a similar stalwart of the squadron, also well into his second tour. A VR officer, Hall had won an 'immediate' DFC in July 1941 during an attack on Aachen. Just short of the target area his aircraft had been 'coned' by around twenty searchlights and spotted by a marauding nightfighter who went in for the kill. His starboard petrol tank was holed and the aircraft took damage to its mainplane, wings, fuselage and the tail. Luckily his air gunner was on the ball and put up a stout defence, and the fighter disappeared. Hall carried on to the target and made four runs at 5,000ft before dropping his bombs. The shortened citation that appeared in the *London Gazette* said that he had displayed 'a high degree of courage and determination on operations which is unsurpassed.'[37]

It was with another stout squadron 'type', and an unusual one at that, that Eric kicked off his heavy bomber tour of duty. William 'Bill' Dierkes was an American from Cincinnati[38] who had crossed over the border into Canada in October 1940 to enlist in the RCAF at Windsor, Ontario. Although in theory too old to train as a pilot (he was then 29), Dierkes somehow managed to circumvent officialdom and headed for the UK both with his pilot's 'wings' and a commission. He flew his first operation in the first week of January 1943, an attack on Berlin, and in very short order his crew built a sound reputation for their tenacity and skill. The accuracy of their bombing was also recognised with a bombing certificate after a particularly successful raid on Milan in February, and they would add four more such documents before becoming tour expired.

On the night of 8/9 April, Eric was detailed to fly with Bill Dierkes as a 'second dickey', a phrase used to describe a 'sprog' captain sent out to learn the ropes from a more experienced skipper prior to being given responsibility for his own crew. While Eric was no stranger to war, the difference between flying a comparatively fast, very low-level bombing attack in daylight in a Fairey Battle and a long, six or seven-hour slog at 18,000ft at night across the cold skies of occupied Europe in a four-engine 'heavy' couldn't be more extreme. That said, nearly all bomber COs insisted that pilots new to a squadron flew a second dickey, no matter how extensive their experience, especially if they had been out of the game for some time or operating in Europe for the first time. Many of the more experienced men in Bomber Command in 1943 had flown their first tour of ops in the Middle East with a different set of dangers and terrain.

Despite his rank, and his flying experience, Eric was to all intents and purposes a novice. Aside from the camaraderie of the squadron, everything was different and strange. In France, briefing prior to an operation was often a hastily arranged affair, with a handful of crews gathered around a table while the CO did his best to give his pilots the best 'gen' available. There was no fixed Time on Target (ToT), no organised take-off en masse, and very little to help them on their way beyond the enthusiasm of their senior officer and the knowledge that their backs were well and truly up against the wall. If you failed to stop the armour, and failed to destroy a particular bridge, there wouldn't be time to have another go the next day. The Panzers would be among you. At Syerston, as with every other Main Force bomber squadron across the East Midlands, Lincolnshire and The Ridings, briefings were now thoroughly organised, disciplined, and large, comprising a level of detail and information that was unimaginable at the start of the war. Eric knew he would be flying that night as he had been given the nod by his flight commander and his name had appeared on the Battle Order, a list of all crews required for operations. Various times were advised for individual briefings given to navigators and captains, ahead of the main briefing at which the whole crew would learn the target. Throughout the morning, information had filtered down from Group to the intelligence officer as to the scale of the attack (e.g a 'Goodwood' was the codeword for a maximum effort requiring as many aircraft as the squadron could muster) followed by a designated H-hour (the time of the attack) together with the route. From that moment on the action started, as the squadron commander, flight commanders, armament officer, navigation officer, signals officer, bombing leader, engineering officer, flying control, photographic section and operations clerks set to work. The target dictated the bomb load, whether GP, high explosives (HEs), incendiaries or perhaps a mix of different types, while the weight of bombs, and commensurately the fuel load, were also a factor of how far the Lancasters had to travel, given that their all-up weight (for a Lancaster Mk1) could not exceed 63,500lbs. Crews quickly learned to guess at the potential target based on this calculation. A heavy bomb load and limited fuel meant a target close to home, perhaps Northern France or the Ruhr. Fewer bombs and more fuel meant a long haul to Berlin or Stettin on the Baltic, or one of the Italian cities of Spezia, Genoa or Milan. Some even got to recognise the codewords. The 'Usual' meant a 4,000-pound 'Cookie' and twelve Small Bomb Containers (SBCs), each SBC loaded with either twenty-four, thirty-pound incendiaries or 236 four-pound incendiaries. 'Arson', perhaps not surprisingly, comprised 14,000-pounds of bombs, all incendiaries, in fourteen SBCs. If the order called for an Abnormal bomb load, the armourers loaded eight one-thousand-pound GP bombs.

The briefing itself was something of a dog and pony show, a performance, but deadly earnest. A series of specialists gave the men the vital information they needed to make it safely there and back. Special attention was paid to the 'Met' man and the weather conditions they could expect en route and over the target. Crews were often more concerned with the expected weather on the return leg, and whether they'd be able to make it back to the station from which they'd left. Any crew that had flown more than a handful of ops would have most likely been diverted at some point to land at an unfamiliar station overnight when fog had prevented a more direct route home.

Similar attention was paid to the intelligence officer, and the reception they could expect from the enemy defences. Nightfighters were well-organised, and morale among the leading 'Experten' ('Experts', a Luftwaffe equivalent of the RAF's 'Aces') was still high. The Germans had extended the depth of their defensive line, known to the Allies as the Kammhuber Line, and similarly increased the calibre of guns to defend their cities. Bomber Command had retaliated with new tactics, including the use of the bomber 'stream' to overwhelm the defences by pushing as many bombers through a single point as quickly as possible, before the Germans had time to get organised. So began a war of measure and counter-measure as the balance steadily tipped in favour of the RAF and the Luftwaffe began to fight what it increasingly learned was a losing battle. But that was for some time in the future; in the here and now, many of the Experten were at the top of their game, and nightfighters something to be genuinely feared.

For Eric's first trip they chose the great inland port of Duisberg, lying at the junction of the Rhine and the River Ruhr, a city with a large population (c440,000) and well known both as a transport hub and the production of coal and steel. As just one region of Germany, the Ruhr produced more steel in a year than the entire annual production of the UK. It was similarly responsible for nearly two thirds of the UK's equivalent coal production and twice its metallurgical coke production. But the true 'uniqueness' of the Ruhr lay in its intricate transport system which comprised not only an elaborate network of railways but also its canals and waterways, with Duisberg at its core. It was a prime target but being in the Ruhr it was often difficult to find, both because of an almost unique microclimate in the area and the artificial conditions created by hundreds of industrial chimneys spilling polluted fumes into the environment. Its environs included a section of the Vereinigte Stahlwerke, the Thyssen Hutte AG, and the world-famous Krupps furnaces at Rheinhausen, on the opposite bank of the river. As one contemporary RAF officer wrote: 'There are armaments works of almost every description, turning out chemicals and their by-products, heavy guns, airscrews, ships' boilers, torpedo nets and gun barrels.'[39]

On their flight out, Eric observed the interactions of the crew with keen and professional interest. Below him, and despite the blackout, there was still the occasional light to be seen as they crossed the coast, and soon they were over another coast where the few lights visible took on a more sinister significance. Eric continued to observe as Dierkes reminded his air gunners to keep a sharp look out for enemy fighters as they neared the target, and the first of a number of searchlights began groping the sky, lighting up small patches of cloud above and beneath them. Eric could also hear the occasional thump as a flak shell exploded a little too close for comfort. Eric had experienced flak before, but nothing quite like this. His pilot, however, flew on unconcerned, save for the difficulty he was having in seeing any of the Pathfinder markers. It was a problem many others were having. With little choice left to him, he used his last navigational 'fix' to determine where they were and when they should be over Duisberg and instructed for the bombs to be released accordingly. Then he headed for home.

While Eric's first operation went off without a hitch, and all of the squadron aircraft returned home safely, post-raid analysis showed that little damage had been done.. Eric followed this raid two nights later flying 'second dickey' to Geoffrey Hall to Frankfurt, where cloud over the target again meant the crews had no real idea where their bombs had fallen. The bombing photographs of every aircraft were said to have shown nothing but cloud. Hall followed Dierkes in reverting to a 'timed run' from an established datum point to release his bombs on what his air bomber hoped should be the target.

In-between these two raids, Eric sat down to catch up with his correspondence. He was assiduous in his letter writing when time allowed, but felt the need to apologise to Clu for not having replied sooner:

> I am perusing yours of 17th March and hope you don't think too badly of me for not writing sooner, but I am operational now, which means I don't get much time. Tonight, I am trying to get up-to-date with a number of letters, so, to cope with the quantity I have to cut down the quality. In other words, I mustn't go on nattering like this, or I shall not write to many people tonight.

Eric was keen to re-assure Clu that he was taking care of his physical wellbeing, and that he'd quickly settled into the familiarity of squadron life. Syerston was close to Eric's old stomping ground. The nearest watering holes were in Newark, which Eric describes simply as 'a dirty little town' with 'some nice pubs' which at least enabled him to partake of one of his favourite pastimes, shove ha'penny. He writes without mentioning the station by name, but referring to Betty's advancing stages of pregnancy and his new-found fitness regime:

> You know about my latest moves as you saw Bet last month, after she had been with me a few days. I understand Bet is 'growing' quite well now, and there is no doubt about it she is as happy and well as ever. This place is very near my last place and quite convenient for getting home when that opportunity arises. I drink very little now though, as this night flying business is very strenuous, especially at the heights we operate. I've been trying to keep fit lately, and even did a cross-country run – the first in my life – three miles without a stop! It took a week for my legs to recover! Nottingham isn't too far – it's a town we knew very well of course. I went in there and saw a show the other evening. This station is next door to my old place when we lived at Radcliffe. What a time ago! And here I am on that same old racket.

While penning this letter, Eric was interrupted by his navigator, Len Hewitt, and encouraged to go for a drink:

> Well, bang goes my correspondence evening! My navigator (a F/O) has just asked me to go and have a beer! Incidentally, my crew consists of

seven, five NCOs. What a family!

This last line is especially interesting as somewhere along the line between leaving HCU and arriving at 61 Squadron, Eric had managed to lose his original rear gunner, Maurice Root-Reed. This may have been by accident or design, probably the former, for Eric would fly with Root-Reed later in his tour. For now, however, he had a new member of the crew defending his tail.

Eric was set to take his crew to attack the major naval base at La Spezia in northern Italy on the night of 13/14 April, with one of the squadron's senior navigators, Robert Adams, as captain.[40] The Lancaster (W4763) developed an electrical fault in the bombing gear, however, and the raid had to be aborted, thus sparing the Italians further misery and destruction, albeit temporarily. He flew a rather more successful trip to Stuttgart, again under the tutelage of Robert Adams, two nights later. In place of Maurice Root-Reed, Herbert Rankin joined the crew in the rear turret. Eric will have been delighted with his little Dubliner, for Rankin was already a highly experienced operator. He had once been in a Lancaster attacked by two nightfighters on the same trip, and with skilful commentary had managed to avoid serious damage. According to the citation for the DFM which followed, he was an airman who 'always inspires confidence in his captain and who never wavered in the face of the strongest anti-aircraft fire.'

It was on the night of 16/17 April that Eric was at last trusted to take the captain's role. The target was the Skoda armaments works in Pilsen, a long and dangerous trip of eight hours or more into the heart of enemy territory and into occupied Czechoslovakia. It was a distance, even as the crow flies, and not allowing for the intricate dog legs now being devised to deceive the enemy defences, of more than 800 miles each way. That alone required an expert feat of navigation simply to find the target, even with Pathfinders to help guide them on their journey.

The squadron put up thirteen aircraft out of a total attacking force of 327 Lancasters and Halifaxes, with Gascoyne-Cecil the first to get away in the late evening. Eric followed a few minutes later, his navigator and flying control logging his take-off time at 21.17hrs. Unusually, Harris, the C-in-C, had chosen a night with a full moon to help with navigation and in identifying the target. It was always a trade-off; a full moon helped the attackers, especially in identifying landmarks that could be fed into the navigator's plot; but it also helped the defenders, for a bomber could be easily picked out in a full moon without the need for any sophisticated radar equipment. The bombers would be brilliantly silhouetted in the night sky.

As it was, Harris' gamble didn't pay off; the raid was little short of a disaster. Since Pilsen was beyond the range of Oboe, Pathfinders were using a different blind bombing device known as H2S to identify and mark the target. H2S was a ground-scanning radar installed on the aircraft and therefore unlimited in range. The radar returns gave the navigator a ghostly image, displayed on a primitive oscilloscope, of the ground below. It was especially good at distinguishing between land and large bodies of water, such as coastlines and lakes. But the flickering and often indeterminate picture required skill, knowledge and luck to interpret, and sets would often be on the blink. It was a science, but not always an exact one, and on this night the marking Pathfinders thought the image on their screens was the Skoda factory when in fact what they were seeing was a lunatic asylum near Dobrany, some seven miles from their target. The sprawling nature of the asylum's buildings were mistaken for a factory. The marking in this case, however, was only intended as a general guide, and Main Force had been instructed to confirm their own view of the target visually before bombing. The fault, therefore, was universal, and out of the 300 or so bombers who claimed to have hit the target, only six had in fact got anywhere near it. The Skoda plant remained intact. Worse, thirty-six bombers were shot down, eleven percent of the attacking force and the highest loss rate suffered by Bomber Command in a Main Force raid up to that point. Gascoyne-Cecil reported seeing one of the PFF aircraft explode right in front of him on the run up to the target, easily identifiable by the mass of multi-coloured fireworks that spat from its dying shell.[41] Eric too reported seeing at least five aircraft shot down around them. He landed at 05.35hrs, one of the first to make it back, the last landing a full hour after the engines on Eric's Lancaster had fallen silent. An hour later and Eric retired to bed, unaware at that point that one of their own squadron aircraft was missing. It was not until late into the same day that Lancaster W4317 with 22-year-old William MacFarlane was confirmed as lost, no communication with the aircraft being received after take-off. It was a bitter blow. MacFarlane had flown thirty operations and was at the end of his tour. His wireless operator had flown fifty, a double tour. Both were scheduled for a well-earned and much-needed rest, but now their rest was permanent.

Eric wrote to Betty the next day, her twenty-fifth birthday. He was far from depressed or downbeat. Before the war he had been something of a pacifist, simply wanting to learn to fly so that he could save up enough money to get married. Now he seemed to be enjoying war, or at least the challenge of such deep penetration attacks:

> The opportunity for writing this has arisen like this. The 'usual' took place last night and I was in bed by 7.30am. I intended to sleep until 4pm but buzzing aeroplanes and the sunlight streaming in forced me to

get up at 12.30. I had lunch and find tonight in a stand down. The flight commander is off, so I am sitting in the office signing passes for the NCOs for the afternoon. They have to have them to get out of camp. So, I'm in the office by myself, enjoying the quiet peace. My eyes are a bit sore with tiredness but I shall sleep well tonight over the proper hours, for a change. Last night, by the way, was a very nice trip. Quite thrilling! What a different chap I am these days! He! he!

As a flight lieutenant, it was not surprising that Eric had been asked to deputise for his immediate 'boss', the flight commander. The flight commander was responsible for ensuring the maximum availability of men and machines when they were needed, and in maintaining the discipline and morale of his men. He would watch for signs of nervous strain and the 'twitch', to head off any potential problems, as well as dealing with the more sundry duties, such as signing a coveted pass for thirsty aircrew and groundcrew to leave the station during a stand-down, usually to head into town for a watered-down pint. In the same letter, aside from referencing a comedy apple sent to him by his mother-in-law, Eric also highlights some of the more practical issues of being a bomber pilot:

D'you know I go seven hours in the air now, without a pee! Getting trained, aren't I! He! he! Ta for the laundry and the funny apple. What a rude looking apple it was! I wonder why Mam insisted on sending it? My love and adoring wishes to my angel on her 25th.

P.S. I do get bum-sore, sitting in the pilot's seat for seven hours! I must try to get hold of an extra comfy cushion. X

The physical and mental challenge of a long trip into enemy territory is brought home in such simple and urbane words. Maintaining a level of concentration for upwards of seven, eight or even nine hours or more took a superhuman effort. Air gunners would create their own routines, scanning particular parts of the sky in sequence, and continuing to do so throughout the flight. They could not afford to relax for a single second, for it could be at that very moment that a nightfighter struck. The Germans had taken to following the bomber stream back to their bases in the north and attacking just as the tired and unwary bomber captains came into land. There was a chemical toilet provided on the aircraft, the Elsan toilet, but it was rarely used. No-one could afford to leave their station unless it was absolutely necessary, least of all the pilot, which is why Eric writes about his newfound level of self-restraint in his letter. Comfort was not a major feature of a bomber crew's life. The mid-upper gunner, for example, had a seat that was not dissimilar to the seat on a playground swing; the flight engineer had a metal seat that folded down and was so uncomfortable that many chose to stand throughout the duration of a flight. The crew, with the exception of the pilot, wore chest-type parachutes. These were effectively in two parts: a harness and a parachute pack. The former was worn, and the second stowed until it was required and then retrieved and clipped to the front of the harness should the order be given to bail out. The pilot, on the other hand, wore a seat-type parachute, acknowledging that in an emergency, the pilot would unlikely have the luxury or the time of making up his own kit. It meant, however, that he had to sit on his 'chute for the whole journey, and the parachute pack was likened by some skippers as the equivalent of sitting on a bag of cement. Little wonder, therefore, that Eric talks of finding a more comfortable cushion!

If Eric thought that the operations would become less arduous, he was very much mistaken. Despite this being the Battle of the Ruhr, in the immediate term Harris had his eyes on other targets, and none of them close by. On 18/19 April, and at the second time of asking, Eric finally bombed La Spezia, an epic trip of more than nine hours. He had the satisfaction of clearly identifying the target visually and attacking from 8,000 feet, obtaining a photograph at the point that his bombs released and in line with operational procedure. Every aircraft was equipped with a camera and a photo flash which were deployed when the bombs fell. Eric had to keep the Lancaster straight and level to get a bombing photograph that was then scrutinised on his return to determine whether he had hit the right target and suggest what damage might have been caused. The best bombing photographs would be sent to group, and it was a source of great pride to every squadron, and every squadron air bomber, if one of their photographs was subsequently picked out for special mention. Eric's Lancaster, W4198, was slightly damaged on landing but quickly repaired.[42]

Two nights later, Eric set out on another long haul, this time to Stettin on the Baltic. He had a different NCO rear gunner, William Crawshaw, while a BBC reporter accompanied one of the other crews. Stettin involved a round-trip of almost 1,300 miles but as the biggest port in the Baltic, and one that served the Nazi capital, it was a target of particular significance. Much of the vital war traffic with neutral Sweden passed through the city, and Harris was determined to interrupt that flow as best he could. It was also a vital supply base for German troops operating in the northern part of the Russian front. Whereas the raid on Pilsen had been a flop, the attack on the centre of Stettin was a complete success. Visibility over the target was variable but the Pathfinder marking extremely accurate. Although unable to see the target, Eric was able to identify a cluster of Green Target Indicators (TIs) at which he aimed, and with thick clouds of smoke rising from the target and the first fires on the ground now beginning to burn he turned for home. One of their number, James Rossignol, failed to return. Although part of the RCAF, he was in fact another American, from Daytona Beach. He had come a long way from the comforting warmth of the Florida sun to lose his life in the freezing bleakness of the Baltic. Eric had known him briefly at HCU.

Eric now settled into the natural rhythm of Main Force raids of the period, punctuating long slogs to the east, or south into Italy, with shorter but no-less dangerous trips to the Happy Valley, as the Ruhr was ironically named. He visited Duisberg (twice), Pilsen (with rather more luck), Dortmund (involving more than 800 aircraft, large parts of the city being devastated) and Düsseldorf. For the Düsseldorf trip he carried his own second dickey, a sprog pilot now benefiting from Eric's experience, though it was not a successful attack. The Syerston Station Commander, Reginald 'Oddy' Odbert went along with Gascoyne-Cecil for the ride and to keep his hand in, a 'station master' who liked to fly when he could. It was ironic that he was killed two months later while on a gunnery demonstration flight. The Wellington in which he was flying fell out of the sky practising a corkscrew manoeuvre as part of a fighter affiliation exercise.

Düsseldorf was again the preferred target on the night of 11/12 June, suffering a frustrating phenomenon known as a 'hang up', when one of the bombs failed to release. This was not an uncommon occurrence, and often the bomb could be jettisoned safely or shaken loose with some gentle aerobatics. If the bomb still steadfastly refused to shift, it was possible to land with it still on board, but it was seldom the preferred option. Everyone had heard stories of the bomb coming loose in the bomb bay as the aircraft landed and exploding and/or causing serious injury and death to an unsuspecting ground crew once the bomb doors were opened. There were protocols and procedures to avoid such things, but mistakes could happen, and occasionally did.

A feature of these trips was the constant rotation of air gunners occupying Eric's rear turret. Stan Mattick joined him for a Duisberg raid on 12/13 May before he was posted out[43] and Thomas Jones, another NCO, took his place for three trips to Essen (27/28 May), Wuppertal (29/30 May) and the trip to Düsseldorf with the recalcitrant bomb release.[44] The attack on Wuppertal was especially satisfying and described by the historians as 'the outstanding success of the Battle of the Ruhr'.[45] The Pathfinder marking was accurate and Main Force bombing bang on the money such that a large fire broke out in the narrow streets of the old part of the town, creating the very first of what would later be recognised as a fire storm, consuming everything in its wake. A bad situation was compounded by the absence of a number of the town's fire and air raid officials who had left for their country homes, the attack coming on a Saturday night. War, it appears, was not to upset their weekend routine.

For his part, Eric enjoyed a particularly successful trip though others were not so fortunate. Thirty-three bombers were shot down, including seven Lancasters, but all the No. 61 Squadron aircraft made it home. Some were lucky to do so, and several reported fighter combats over or near the target area. One NCO pilot was coned, and landed with flak damage to his bomb doors, fuselage and tail, obliging him to jettison his bombs. Eric too was shot at while crossing the English coast – by his own side!

While Main Force went about its nightly duties in the second quarter of 1943, a very 'special' squadron, No. 617, had been formed within No. 5 Group under the command of Guy Gibson to attack certain critical dam structures that were essential for supplying water to the industrial Ruhr. Eric had more than a passing interest in its success, given that several of the aircrew had been poached from No. 61 Squadron before and during his time there. He was also to follow in the footsteps of the mercurial Gibson and know something of his last operation and his untimely and many would say unnecessary and thoroughly avoidable death.

Meanwhile, however, and with the Allied army's success in North Africa in the winter of 1942/43, came the capture of several new airfields, notably Maison Blanche in Algeria. This is turn allowed Harris to experiment with a new form of bombing operation that would not only fox the Germans entirely but, if successful, could provide a legitimate opportunity to attack the enemy from a direction they would least expect. The target chosen for his experiment was the Zeppelin works at Friedrichshafen on the shores of Lake Constance. The attack was in fact the brainchild of Sir Ralph Cochrane, AOC No. 5 Group, no doubt flushed by the success of the Dams raid just a few weeks earlier. He was at the time and subsequently Harris' blue-eyed boy and Harris rewarded Cochrane's zest for experimentation and thinking outside the box with his full support.

Days before the operation, codenamed 'Bellicose', Eric and the four other captains selected for the attack had undertaken a series of specialist exercises at the bombing range in Wainfleet, Lincolnshire. There was also more than a little excitement when asked to draw tropical kit from the stores, including a quantity of 'topees' – ancient-looking Pith helmets left over from the Habbaniya campaign.

The attack was an all-5 Group affair involving sixty aircraft in two waves, including five from No. 61 Squadron. It was led by Leonard Slee. Slee, a group captain, was no stranger to specialist raids, having won the Distinguished Service Order (DSO) for his part in the daylight attack on Le Creusot the year before. On the outward leg, however, Slee's Lancaster developed engine trouble, probably as the result of flak, and his place was taken by his deputy, the OC No. 467 Squadron Cosme Gomm.

On approaching the target, the German defenders put up an intense barrage of flak, so intense that the deputy decided to abandon the plan to go in low and bomb from between 10,000ft and 15,000ft. Unfortunately, the wind at height was much stronger than forecast, and several of the bombers had trouble in obeying their leader's instruction. Eric managed to drop his bombs on some well-placed green markers without particular difficulty and was pleased to see the bombs burst on the target and surrounding roads. Others were not so lucky, either being coned by searchlights or engaged by flak, and one suffered a hang up not just from one of his bombs, but almost half his load. They left the scene, however, with fires well ablaze and no doubt surprised later to discover that many of their bombs had missed completely.

Immediately after dropping his bombs and closing the bomb bay doors, Eric opened the throttles and continued flying straight ahead beyond the target zone. Avoiding Swiss airspace, he headed over the Alps and into Italy before heading southwest across the Mediterranean to the coast of North Africa. It was a move that completely outsmarted the Germans. Their nightfighters had gathered to attack the returning bombers where they expected them to be and not where they ended up, and as a result not a single Lancaster was lost, or fighter encountered. Some were hit by flak and many only just made it to Algeria with the very last drop of fuel in their tanks. Eric was one of them, after an epic flight of exactly ten hours, the latter stages in the sweltering heat that led him and his crew to shed much of the flying gear they were wearing.

They arrived over Maison Blanche to find the airfield shrouded in mist. Encouraged by the US Controller to 'come on in' without identifying which specific aircraft he was talking to, Eric was alarmed to see at least two other aircraft attempting to land with him at the same time. Even when he did land and taxi, there was very nearly a collision as yet another Lancaster passed by his nose. It was something of a relief when he finally brought the aircraft to a standstill and switched off, the engines still popping and crackling in the heat.

Eric and his crew enjoyed a few days in the beautiful sunshine living under canvas and a night out on the town in Algiers while a mixed bag of groundcrew struggled with limited equipment and resources to prepare the Lancasters for the return trip. Flight engineers helped where they could, sweating and swearing away in the unfamiliar heat, to make do and mend where possible despite the uncomfortable conditions. Three nights later, fifty-two Lancasters from the original force (some had been damaged beyond immediate repair on landing or lacked the parts to be fixed in time) repeated the trick by bombing La Spezia before returning home, again without loss. Very little damage was claimed, which is perhaps not surprising given the somewhat chaotic arrangements that left some of the bombers with no bombs and only a handful of flares that they attached with bits of wire to the bomb bay. Alfred Raphael, a squadron leader with No. 467 Squadron later reported: 'Suggest that two or three specialists be sent out in advance if the same sort of thing is to be avoided in the future!'. Eric was similarly a little underwhelmed by the organisation at Maison Blanche and criticised the 'rush briefing.' Three out of the four No. 61 Squadron aircraft that made the return attack suffered from hang ups. Eric arrived back at Syerston at 04.35hrs on the morning of 24 June. It is not reported whether he or others within their tiny force followed the lead of other crews by returning with their aircraft loaded with grapes, bananas, and other such exotic fruits that war-torn Britain had long ago forgotten. Eric was, however, interviewed on his return by one of the national newspapers:

> The heat was terrific as we flew south. Most of us took off our flying clothes and some put on our topees before we got out of the planes. We all had our tropical kit with us. We saw no Italian or German fighters.

Allowed only a brief period of respite, Eric was once again on the Battle Order for an attack on Gelsenkirchen on 25/26 June, noteworthy for being led by Wing Commander Penman. Officers Commanding bomber squadrons were limited in their operational flying, and the good ones tended to pick the more difficult trips with which to show their solidarity with their crews. Gelsenkirchen was certainly one of those. It was also noteworthy not for Eric's part in it, but rather the fate that befell one of his fellow pilots, David Pearce. Pearce had just dropped his bombs and was heading for home when his Lancaster was hit by flak, knocking out the port outer engine. Not in any immediate danger Pearce managed to make the English coast before the engine caught fire at which point he ordered the crew to bail out. Satisfied that his crew had escaped, and now down to 1,000ft, Pearce jumped from the aircraft himself and landed safely in a field, watching as he came down his Lancaster crash into the ground around 200-yards away. Sadly, and for reasons unknown, the mid upper gunner failed to make it out of the aircraft, and the navigator could not be found, despite his harness and parachute being recovered.[46]

Eric did not write about his adventures in the sun, nor did he speak of the loss of any squadron crews. He was meant to have been on the trip to Hamburg on 24/25 July – important because it was the RAF's first use of thin strips of aluminium foil known as 'Window' which played havoc with German radar defences – but his Lancaster developed a fault, and he didn't take off. He did make it to Essen the next night, however, with the squadron Gunnery Leader, Charles Ingham DFC, in the rear turret.

With Betty now eight months pregnant, the recently promoted Squadron Leader Benjamin penned a new verse to his unborn baby on 20 July:

> Before its baby eyelids open to a scarred
> and shattered world; before those precious
> eardrums vibrate to the wicked
> blare of battle; before this contaminated
> air fans those tiny nostrils and minute
> lungs expand to inhale its wickedness;
> before we hear a cry from pure, virgin lips
> and infant arms reach out to resist
> these daily enemies;
> - before all this, - let us pray.
> Let us pray for the blessing of God, so
> that our little one will have the strength
> to fight all manner of evil which
> comes its way.

Three and a half weeks later, on 17 August 1943, Betty gave birth to a girl at a Maternity Home for Officers' wives, Fulmer Chase, near Stoke Poges in Buckinghamshire.[47]

Eric took out his small Stationery Office book in which he captured his thoughts to write the final piece of his poem about his daughter's birth:

> On this day - in the morning - she came into
> the world - Jeannie.
> We give thanks
> To God for this happy deliverance – there
> was never a greater day.

The couple chose the name Jeannie because of a popular song of the time called 'I dream of Jeannie with the light brown hair,' and it was Eric's favourite. Soon after, Betty's two sisters, Winnie and Claudia, cycled from Twickenham to Fulmer to see their niece, the first grandchild for Betty's parents. After a difficult birth, Betty spent a further two weeks in a convalescent home nearby before going home to her parents in Teddington, but as yet unable to see her husband and share their new-found joy.

Jeannie's arrival, and the promise and hope of a new life, contrasted starkly with one of the worst periods in No. 61 Squadron's history. Having lost three captains in the first week of the month, in a 72-hour period between 15 – 18 August they lost a further seven aircraft. Forty-nine men in the prime of life either killed, captured or on the run. Four of those aircraft were shot down during the famous attack on the rocket research establishment at Peenemünde on the night Jeannie was born. Among the skippers missing was Thomas Stewart of the Royal New Zealand Air Force (RNZAF), a flight lieutenant coming towards the end of his second tour and who already had the DFM as testament to his first. Remarkably he survived to see out the war in a prisoner-of-war camp. The situation would get worse before it got any better. They lost another crew on the night of 22/23 and by the end of the month had thirteen crews reported missing, more than the combined total of losses reported over the next four months. The final tragedy was the loss of 27-year-old Canadian Dennis Wellburn DFC, a recently appointed squadron leader, killed in a collision on his return from Berlin.

Although not on leave, Eric managed to avoid the disasters that befell others and it was not until later in the month that he was again required to operate, by which time he was now a flight commander. Harris was still pressing home the temporary advantage he had in numbers and technical superiority and was momentarily but necessarily side-tracked by diverting some of his force to attack targets in Italy to hasten that country's surrender. (It worked. Italy surrendered on 8 September). His thinking, however, had moved on from the Ruhr and he now had his sights set firmly on the Big City itself, Berlin, with an ambitious plan to bring the Germans to their knees by knocking out their capital.

As the capital of the Reich, and 'the great administrative centre of Hitlerism'[48], Berlin held both emotional and political significance. But it also had numerous war industries, including the 'big five' comprising the Alkett factory in Spandau which produced half of the German army's field artillery; the Borsigwerken making rolling stock and locomotives; the DWM and DIW combines, both producing large quantities of small arms and ammunition; and Siemens, the electrical giant, which so dominated the city that it had its own self-contained 'Siemensstadt'. Berlin was also home to at least ten AEG factories, three BMW and Daimler Benz motor factories, and three Henschel and Dornier aircraft factories, as well as a plethora of smaller firms making everything from precision lenses to specialist communications. It was also an important inland port, connected by canals and waterways with all parts of Germany.[49]

Eric had the satisfaction of taking part in one of the first of these raids[50] but instead of his usual crew he took another crew altogether. The only familiar face was that of Maurice Root-Reed, the air gunner with whom he had parted company soon after joining the squadron.

It was a colossal raid, one of the biggest ever mounted on the Nazi stronghold, and unusual in that it was directed by a Master Bomber, the mercurial Johnny Fauquier, widely regarded as one of the best bomber commanders of the war. Despite Fauquier's best efforts, and the report of the OC No. 61 Squadron who also described the attack as 'an excellent show', the results didn't quite match the billing. Most of the bombs fell outside of the city but casualties among the civilian population were heavy, largely because so many had failed to take cover. But the damage came at a high cost to Bomber Command. It suffered the greatest loss of aircraft in a single night up to that point in the war. Twenty three Halifaxes, seventeen Lancasters and sixteen Stirlings failed to return. With a loss rate approaching eight percent, the numbers were simply not sustainable, and the bomber boys knew it. If such rates were to continue, the mathematics told them that none of them would survive.

On the night of 3/4 September 1943, Eric very nearly added to those sombre statistics. His regular crew was accompanied by a second dickey, Frank O'Malley[51], and Joseph Frawley in the mid upper turret was partnered with Leonard Say in the rear. Say was the regular rear gunner of the CO, Penman, and had recently been commissioned. He obviously knew his stuff, because very few air gunners made it to become officers, and perhaps fewer still to clock up two tours. He'd flown his first sortie back in 1941, as the regular air gunner to Rupert Gascoyne-Cecil, and had survived the full gambit of experiences, from beating off a fighter attack over Pilsen to being rendered unconscious when his aircraft was struck by lightning!

Unusually, the planners for this particular raid had opted for a straight 350-mile run to the target over the Dutch coast, which foxed the Germans into thinking it had to be a ruse. It was a considerable risk, and the bombers were lucky. The attacking force also had further luck over the target, as the forecasted cloud cleared, allowing the Pathfinders to mark the aiming point with noteworthy accuracy and keep the Target Indicators regularly 'backed up'. With Lancasters dotted about and jinking all over the sky, some clearly visible, Eric started his bombing run and was happy to see a large explosion below him, shortly after making his attack. With the bomb doors closed and the obligatory photograph taken, Eric turned due north where the planners had controversially routed the Main Force return such that it infringed Swedish airspace. The Swedes opened fire, more for show than with any real intent, the flak exploding several thousand feet below and of no consequence to the bombers. Another letter of complaint from the Swedish authorities was swift in coming for the deliberate violation of its airspace. It was another letter that was kicked into the diplomatic long grass.

Eric landed back at base after an exhausting eight-hour slog and reported 'surprisingly good results' to the Intelligence Officer. Indeed, the raid had been a success, with several important factories hit, among them Siemens and AEG. The house of General Guderian, one of the most senior German army commanders and pioneer of the Blitzkrieg idea, was also destroyed.

In reply, the Germans accounted for twenty Lancasters, and it might have been twenty-one had it not been for the skill and experience of Eric's gunners. They fought off multiple, determined attacks by two Junkers 88s, and their Lancaster (JB137, F Freddie) was badly shot up. It was Say's fifty-second and final trip, and very nearly his last. He was awarded the DFC to add to the DFM he'd won on completion of his first tour.[52]

There was personal recognition too for Eric in the first week of September with the award of the DFC for a sustained period of bravery in air operations, and undoubtedly for his part in bringing his damaged bomber back from Berlin. Coincidentally the announcement appeared in the same issue of the *London Gazette* (10 September 1943) as that of a similar award to his OC, Bill Penman. It was with considerable pride that he stitched the distinctive purple and white diagonal ribbon on his tunic beneath his pilot's wings, a worthy and visible symbol of his contribution and sacrifice during three hard years of war.

Understandably, Eric makes no mention of the fighter attack in any of his letters home. A week after his wife had the pleasure of seeing her husband's name in the *Gazette*, she was at last able to see him in person, and Eric was able to greet his baby daughter. He was now the proud Daddy he'd so wanted to be and adored every moment he spent with his new family. To celebrate the reunion, he and Betty arranged for some professional photographs to be taken to capture their precious time together. All too soon, however, his leave was over, and he was heading back to the realities of war.

The 'realities' included bearing witness to a truly shocking incident on the squadron one cold autumnal morning when the men were ordered on parade. Forming something of a loose square (aircrew were not renowned for their drill!), a bare-headed sergeant was marched out in front of them, a Service policeman on either side. Standing to attention, a senior officer approached and proceeded to melodramatically tear off the sergeant's flying brevet, stripes and buttons. Cruelly denuded of all rank and dignity, the man was marched off the parade ground to the mournful beat of a drum to an uncertain but doubtless unpleasant future. He had intentionally or otherwise forfeited the confidence of his commanding officer, a crime more commonly known as Lacking Moral Fibre (LMF). Ritual humiliation was the best way, so some officers believed, to prevent the 'disease' from spreading.

With his responsibilities at home and on the squadron, Eric was now in sight of completing his tour of duty, and the welcome promise of at least six-months' rest that would follow. Thoughts began to form in his mind as to what he might do next, but for now he had to concentrate on the task in hand. He took his usual crew, with Maurice Root-Reed in the tail, to Munich at the start of October, flying in Lancaster JB138. Christened 'Just Jane' after the famous cartoon strip of the era, Jane was very much a lucky Lancaster, notching up more than one hundred operations and becoming something of a celebrity in her own right. She certainly proved lucky for Eric, bringing him home in safety despite significant fighter activity circling over the city ahead of the attack and heavy flak on the run up to the target. The fighters accounted for Eric's fellow flight commander, Bryce Cousens who had only been on the squadron for a couple of weeks and was on his fifth operation. (He later became editor of the Sagan newspaper for fellow PoWs.)

It was on the following raid, however, that tragedy once again befell the squadron when Wing Commander Penman failed to return. The target was Kassel, and the attack did not go according to plan. As crews returned to be debriefed by the intelligence officers, they were asked the usual questions about what they'd seen to and from the target, the intensity of the enemy defences, where they had seen an aircraft shot down and at what time. When the wingco didn't show, word got around the station within minutes. He had been a popular leader, never one to shirk his responsibilities, tough but fair, and difficult to replace. Notified of his promotion to group captain and due to take up the rank the following day, many of his men had thought him indestructible, and yet the air war had once again proven that experience could only take you so far. Luck still had a huge part to play. His death held even more significance for Eric because not only had he lost a commanding officer who he respected, but he'd also lost his flight engineer (Ken Stephenson) and his original rear gunner (Maurice Root-Reed) who'd been part of Penman's crew that night. Stephenson had only recently been commissioned, a rare accolade for his 'trade'. Root-Reed was only three trips short of completing his tour.

Penman's death led to an inevitable changing of the guard at No. 61 Squadron. A new man, Reginald Stidolph, arrived to take command and a few weeks later orders were received for the Squadron to move to RAF Skellingthorpe, a disruption that Eric didn't need when only a handful of trips away from safety. The pace and frequency of operations he'd experienced when he'd first arrived had slackened considerably, and after six months at Syerston the place had become like home. He would have been happy to see out his tour there but now had to up-sticks and head slightly north to another unfamiliar station built specially for the war. He also had to say goodbye to his contemporaries in 106, for now they would be partnered with a different squadron, No. 50 Squadron, who had been resident since the airfield opened for business in 1941.

Stidolph was also something of an unknown quantity, and there were few similarities with the man he replaced. He was regular air force, having joined the RAF on a short service commission in 1936, but beyond that the two men had little in common. Stidolph was from Southern Rhodesia and had been a bomber boy all of his service life. He'd served with distinction in North Africa and Burma with No. 113 Squadron until the squadron was pulled out of the line ahead of the Japanese advance. No-one doubted his courage but as with any new CO, he had to prove himself in the eyes of his men. Putting himself on the Battle Order within 24-hours of his arrival on the squadron was a promising start.

Just before the squadron moved, one of their number pulled off a remarkable feat of airmanship that earned him the highest award for gallantry, the Victoria Cross. Bill Reid, a young Scot, had arrived at Syerston in the first week of September and quickly made an impression with Eric and his fellow senior officers for his quiet determination and reliability as a bomber captain. On the night of 3/4 November he had been one of the crews selected for an attack on Düsseldorf, but over the Dutch coast his Lancaster was intercepted by a twin-engine nightfighter whose cannon shells shattered the Lancaster's Perspex canopy which exploded in a blinding flash. Reid was aware that he had been wounded, shards of Perspex had scratched at his face but mercifully missed his eyes, but of more concern was a wound to his shoulder which meant he was losing blood. Pressing on to the target, and with the wind lashing through the shattered windscreen and blood pouring down his face, Reid had only one thought and that was to complete his mission; to turn back and fly against the stream, he calculated, held greater risk.

In assessing the damage, however, the aircraft was in a parlous state. Both turrets had been hit, the communication and compass were out of action, and the elevator trimming tabs u/s which meant the Lancaster became increasingly difficult to handle. Then they were attacked again, this time by a Focke-Wulf Fw190 which raked the already-damaged aircraft from stem to stern, killing the navigator outright and fatally wounding the wireless operator. The flight engineer was also hit, but despite his own wounds helped his captain regain control of the aircraft and provide emergency oxygen since the standard system was put out of action. Still refusing to turn back, Reid continued to the target and dropped his bombs before steering north to avoid the worst of the enemy defences.

Using the pole star and the moon to guide him, he headed for home, growing increasingly weak from loss of blood and exhausted from the physical effort of keeping the Lancaster in some sort of flying condition.

He eventually put the aircraft down at the first airfield he saw, the undercarriage collapsing as the aircraft touched the runway and the battered body of the Lancaster sliding along the ground before finally coming to a halt in a cloud of mud and debris. The airfield was RAF Shipdham, base for the 44th Bombardment Group of the USAAF, and he and his surviving crew were immediately taken into their care. When the AOC of No. 5 Group heard the story he visited Reid in hospital and promptly recommended the survivors for gallantry awards which included the Victoria Cross for Bill Reid and a Conspicuous Gallantry Medal for his doughty flight engineer, James Norris.

The attack on Bill Reid's aircraft reveals a notable change in tactics by the German defenders. Alongside aircraft guided to their targets by ground controllers there were also those of a more freelance nature, the so-called 'wild boars', who loitered in the target area, waiting for their prey to appear. As the autumn turned to winter, and the C-in-C Bomber Command mounted the first of a series of heavy raids on Berlin, so too were the German nightfighters again in the ascendancy.

The main Battle of Berlin, as it was called, opened on the night of 18/19 November with a comparatively modest raid comprising 440 bombers. The second raid a few nights later was more impressive, although the target was cloud covered and Eric and the returning crews could only estimate the damage they had done. They had aimed at 'sky markers' in a technique known as 'Wanganui'. When the Pathfinders could not visually identify the aiming point, they used their blind bombing aids to 'see' the target and pick a point in the clouds for Main Force to aim at to hit the target below. It was a tactic that was rarely preferred but surprisingly effective. A third raid had similar issues, but was noteworthy for the success of British efforts to fool the enemy ground controllers by broadcasting fake instructions of their own.

The second attack, on the night of 22/23 November, proved to be Eric's final flight with No. 61 Squadron and the end of his tour. Again, it was in 'Just Jane' and again it was a mixed crew. With Ken Stephenson and Maurice Root-Reed now sadly gone, he had a 'spare' flight engineer, Arthur Woodvine, and rear gunner (Sergeant H F Blore) as well as an unfamiliar face occupying the mid-upper turret, Reginald Blagdon. Eric had little to report from the raid other than seeing a large explosion in the target area, an event also remembered by other crews on their return to base.

A few days later, and news spread across Skellingthorpe that a party of reporters and cameramen were coming and wanted to talk to them. Eric and a large group of No. 61 and No. 50 Squadron aircrew gathered to be interviewed by a journalist from *Pathé News* who invited the men to recount their recent experiences. Reg Stidolph took centre stage at the microphone, introducing 'his' three squadron leaders to share their impressions.

In a stirring piece of newsreel footage, the camera pans across a sea of smiling faces as the announcer proclaims:

> These are just a few of the great army of airmen who took part in the three great saturation attacks on the German capital. And there's no sight of strain after completing the most dangerous flight in the world.

Pointing to the nose art on the Lancaster, the announcer continues:

> You can see from the bomb design how many flights this plane has made over enemy territory, including two in daylight, and as you see it's an empire affair.

The camera pans to show different airmen proudly wearing the shoulder flashes of Canada, Rhodesia, New Zealand, Australia.

> Let's listen to some of the men who have been pounding Berlin with a British variety of a Blitz.

The first to speak, is Wing Commander Stidolph:

> I took part in the first of these three raids, and found Berlin very heavily defended, the trip was a fairly easy one, and we saw one of Germany's much-vaunted 'new weapons', which is a rocket shell. It did not appear very effective, and I don't think it will cause us much trouble.

Stidolph's remarks are interesting for he highlights a phenomenon that troubled a number of crews at the time, namely the suggestion that the Germans had some kind of 'wonder weapon' designed specifically to destroy Allied bombers at height. Often referred to in contemporary accounts as a 'scarecrow', there was no such weapon in existence. What the aircrew were actually seeing was their own aircraft exploding. The wing commander then introduces Squadron Leader Pullen, a flight commander with No. 50 Squadron.[53] Pullen says:

> I thought it was a very quiet trip, we had no bother at all, we were right over the centre of Berlin before they started throwing up the flak at us, but there was no trouble as far as we were concerned although we did see one or two people getting shot up.

Stidolph then turns to Eric, introducing him as taking part in the second and greatest of these three raids. In his somewhat self-effacing account in front of the camera Eric recalls with some empathy the fear of those in the planes below, possibly also referring to the population he was bombing:

> Of course, the second raid was noted for the terrific explosion we've all heard about. It certainly was a big explosion. I remember one on the Hanover trip but that didn't compare in the least with this great flash we saw coming under the clouds. I looked down and I could see Lancasters crawling across the clouds, silhouetted against them. It really must have been a very frightening thing down below.

Standing alongside Eric as he speaks is his navigator, Len Hewitt. Introduced as having flown with Squadron Leader Benjamin, Len is described by his OC as 'one of our promising young navigators'[54]:

> I was on two of these three trips, Sir, and navigation was rather more difficult than usual with bags of cloud all the way to the target. So I was on Dead Reckoning, and we rely entirely on our pilots flying the course that we give them, and pretty good, accurate flying indeed.
> What does help you in these big raids, if you don't see a lot of your own aircraft around you at any time, then you know you're off track and you'd better do something about it quick.

Eric then takes it upon himself to introduce his friend, Squadron Leader E.H 'Jimmy' Moss, who before the war had been a teacher at Radley, and invites him to say something about the third trip that he was on:

> We did have a few fighters around on our trip, but the actual flak over Berlin was very small indeed. We saw very little of it. We saw three or four fighters ourselves. The cloud was much thinner than the previous two raids, but one thing I did notice was the vicious way in which every German town now seems to throw up flak indiscriminately. They all look as though they are absolutely scared stiff of having anyone anywhere near them.

The announcer concludes by saying that the men 'did a grand job' and reminding the audience of the words of the C-in-C Sir Arthur Harris a year earlier when he dismissed those who said that a war could never be won by bombing alone by retorting: 'It has never been tried' and that Germany would provide 'an interesting initial experiment'.

It seems a fitting and satisfactory way for Eric to conclude his first full operational tour. When the newsreel was screened in the local cinema at Twickenham, Betty's sister Winnie had to restrain herself from standing up and shouting proudly, 'That's my brother-in-law!'

Eric (left) and two of his brothers, Ernest (front) and Leslie. An older brother, Albert, died in a road accident.

(All photographs in the picture section, unless stated otherwise, are credited to Jeannie Benjamin)

Winnie, Betty, Claud and Desmond.

Fledgling pilot while being trained at White Waltham.

Holidaying on the Isle of Wight in more peaceful days.

Sergeant pilot Eric Benjamin with his recently awarded 'wings', and the image on the front cover of *The Aeroplane* which prompted Eric to write to De Havilland. (Aeroplane Monthly)

Top left: The newly-commissioned Pilot Officer Eric Benjamin.

Above: Eric and Betty (standing right) with (from the left standing) Alf, Winnie, Desmond and Claud. Seated at the front, Betty's parents, 'Mam' and 'Pop'.

Left: Eric with the aircraft he would fly on his first operation, the Fairey Battle.

Eric with the crew of his Fairey Battle — his observer (left) and wireless operator/air gunner.

Above: Eric's aircraft after he was obliged to land in order to save his wounded air gunner (Bundesarchiv).

Right: Eric with a bandaged hand, the result of a bad crash.

Above: Eric takes centre stage to describe his part in a raid on Berlin. (Benjamin family archive)

Left: The wedding that never was attracted considerable press attention.

Below: The Sunday Pictorial carried the headline 'The Bride in Green'.

Cutting the cake on the wedding day that wasn't!

The happy couple, having finally tied the knot.

Above: Lancaster W4277 of No. 61 Squadron – missing over Kassel one night in October, with Wing Commander Penman at the controls. With Penman that night were Eric's rear gunner and flight engineer. (Alex Root Reed).

Below left: Relaxing at Enville while teaching others how to fly.

Below right: 'Jimmy' Moss, who before the war had been at teacher at Radley. (Radley College archive).

Above: Maurice Root-Reed (second from left) who unusually for an air gunner was commissioned. (Credit – Alex Root Reed).

Below left: Bill Penman - first among 'the nice types' Eric met on his arrival at Syerston (Friends of RAF Skellingthorpe).

Below centre: Reginald Stidolph – who took over from Bill Penman as CO of No. 61 Squadron towards the end of Eric's Lancaster tour. (Anthony Stidolph)

Below right: Reg Stidolph in more peaceful times. (Anthony Stidolph)

Above: Relaxing in the garden at 23 Mays Road, Teddington in the summer of 1944, prior to joining 54 Base.

Right: Like most pilots, Eric enjoyed fast cars, and his incredible pipe, which he was always forgetting!

 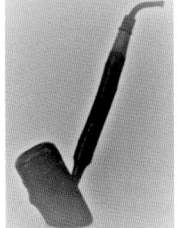

Eric's bravery was recognised with the award of the DFC and Bar.

Left: Father and daughter on a day out at Garrick's Villa, Richmond upon Thames.

Bottom left: Eric's actual silk map which aircrew carried as part of their escape kit.

Bottom right: Eric's epaulette - a Master Bomber warranted a wing commander's rank, though it took some time in coming.

Above: Proud squadron leader and proud father.

Right: The only photograph of the whole family, taken on Eric's last day of leave, i.e. the day before he was killed. Betty was disappointed that Eric was in his shirt sleeves.

Below: Fulmer Chase was a maternity hospital reserved for officers' wives of modest means.

The first, temporary cross to mark Eric's grave, in the town of Colditz, near the castle.

Until we meet again. Betty, Jeanne (sic) and Sally.

Eric's last letter.

Jeannie Benjamin and Fraser Muir, who remembers hearing Eric's last words as he was shot down.

Jeannie pays her respects at her father's grave.

Chapter Five

A Third Ring, a Baby, a DFC and a Bar

Eric and Betty were together on Christmas Day, 1943, spending a blissfully happy time proudly showing off their four-month-old daughter to members of both families. Betty's parents, 'Mam' and 'Pop' and Eric's mother Beatrice doted on little Jeannie, although for some reason Beatrice insisted on calling Jeannie by her middle name Susan, a very popular name at the time. Even Eric began to defer to his mother's preference, albeit briefly.

Having completed his tour Eric was now entitled to a period of 'rest', though the term is somewhat misleading. While the word may have had connotations of rest and recuperation, in effect all it meant was that Eric would not be operating. 'Rest' would be spent on some other duty, perhaps instructing, where his real-world experience could be put to best use training others.

Indeed, it was as an instructor that Eric spent the vast majority of the next few months, being posted out of No. 61 Squadron formally on the week ending 5 December 1943 into the care of No. 5 Group Aircrew School. Of his original crew, they were similarly posted out on completion of their tour, as instructors: Fred Steed to No. 16 OTU and Richard Dinsdale to No. 17 OTU. He would meet Len in training.

Throughout this time, and perhaps reflecting the hours Eric now had to himself compared to when he was operating, he kept up a prolific flow of correspondence with Betty. A few days after Christmas, while based at Scampton, Eric wrote a letter which is the only one to reference Jeannie as Sue:

Sue must be cooing and looking up at you, at this moment. Lovely.
I don't want to bore you by saying I'm pretty browned off with this job. You don't want to hear that, do you. I just wasn't interested, today, and didn't do a spot of work. I got a few things straightened out – wrote to Des, set up your lovely picture and the calendar and clock. What I

should like very much, now, is a good night's rest.

Well, you angel! My goodness! Bit staccato, am I not! You know what I want to say, though - this letter-writing business is so funny – maybe I'll look back on this one, some day, and laugh at myself. Not that one's feelings change, but the mind becomes older with us. The foundation is always there – that never changes. If I have to put a literal translation on that, my dear, it means my love for you has always been the same. It was a beautiful leave, my darling.

The following day, 30 December, Eric wrote to Betty again. He was still enjoying his brief moment of *Pathé* newsreel fame and was delighted that one of their friends had managed to secure a cutting from the film in which Eric featured. (After the war Betty proudly pasted one of the prints from the newsreel into the family album.)

With the New Year came some uncertainty. While relieved to be no longer risking his neck, night after night, over Germany, he was keen to be doing something worthwhile to keep him occupied. He was acutely aware of the men he left behind, and the battle they were now enduring in a terrifying war of attrition with their Luftwaffe foes. He may have been experiencing a bout of survivor's guilt; he was certainly bored. As well as their written correspondence, Eric and Betty were now able to speak together regularly on the phone. Betty would walk up to the end of Mays Road, turn left and walk another 200 yards along Teddington High Street and cross over the road where there was a public phone box. She would have the requisite number of old pennies in her hand and at a pre-arranged time in the early evening they would speak for a few minutes until the money ran out. At the end of Eric's next letter, underneath the usual seven kisses there was now an extra one for his daughter.

> I've got nothing to say – I'm not the busy man I was at Syerston or Skelling – quite the contrary – I've got nothing to do. I pass the time from 9 till 4, somehow. My evenings are busy, though! I'm doing a little private work and the time goes pretty quickly. There's a S/L here, who is very friendly and we have many a natter in the evening, over the odd beer. He wants me to join him at the Station cinema, tonight. It's a pretty deadly place, but I might as well go.

Eric kept himself busy by drawing, painting and writing, referring to it as his 'private work.' He was also an avid reader and was keen to start *A Tale of Two Cities* which he had recently acquired. Betty was still on maternity leave and hoping that the Labour Exchange did not call her back to her work at the National Physical Laboratory too soon. Eric expressed a similar sentiment in his next letter, keen to allay any fears that Betty may have had, that his boredom may lead him to do something rash:

> I hope the Labour Exchange don't expect you to go to work soon! What a shock! I'm not too browned off at my work, now, as I've found a little to do! I've got another course to look after, tomorrow.

Eric sent his 'private work' to Betty and was now looking forward to training as a flying instructor.

> I think I shall be leaving here next Sunday! (for instructional duty). This is the story. As I thought, we flying aces are not being kept on this racket very long and I went for an interview with an air commodore today. A very pleasant chap whom I know a little and he wanted to know what I would like to do. There is little option, of course, but flying instruction, and I pointed out I would like to do the instructor's course. You see, if I'm going to make anything at this racket after the war, I want to get all the Gen! Having got the 'Nav.' ticket, already, I shall be a gen man with a 'flying' instructor's ticket, also. So I think I'm starting my course next Sunday and it takes place down south not too far from Reading. I expect to be able to get home from there for the odd 24 hours. (The course is about 5 weeks.) I don't think there's a chance of getting home before I leave here.

Eric's words reveal more than he was simply excited by additional training to relieve the boredom. They suggest he was looking to the future, and perhaps a longer-term career in the RAF when the war was over, with a permanent commission. The more skills he acquired, the more robust his case would become, and many of his contemporaries were thinking along similar lines.

Eric's interview with the air commodore was at RAF Swinderby, where he bumped into his old pal, Squadron Leader 'Jimmy' Moss:

> I saw Mossy at Swinderby, where I had the interview, today. He was there on a short flight-commanders' course. I saw a lot of old faces, there, - chaps I've met in training, going right back to Bobbington. But there I go! – I've done enough reminiscing!

It was the last time he saw his good friend. Moss was shot down and killed three months later in a disastrous attack on Nuremberg in which the RAF lost in one night more aircrew than had been killed in Fighter Command in the entire Battle of Britain.[55]

Betty was also planning for the future, and with a similarly pragmatic mind. She had starting enquiring into life insurance. Eric knew something about the insurance business. It had been his occupation in civvy street, and he was far from impressed with the advice his wife had been given:

> In answer to the insurance, you can tell him I don't believe in it! If he wants to know any more, tell him to join a company such as the London & Lancashire! He!
>
> In actual fact, though, he's a bl---- liar! The sum assured is £88 for death other than through flying and only £30 for other causes! The whole deal is monstrous and Post Office Savings Certificates are the best investment any time! And wouldn't it be foolish if I didn't take out a policy with my own company if I wanted to at all, when they offer me such a handsome commission! Haw! haw! to your insurance man and tell him to go to war! The old shark! Take it from me, all insurance narks are sharks! You've only got to look at the profits of insurance companies.

Eric wrote to Betty from Scampton on 15 January 1944, hoping for his next posting to come through and for his interview with the air commodore to pay dividends. He was not hopeful that it would come any time soon:

> The Wing Commander here is an awkward customer and I cannot get away until my relief comes. As my relief doesn't arrive until the 17th and my course starts on the 18th, I can't see how things will work out. I shall have to go to Swinderby on the 16th and leave there on the 17th, so I expect I shall be away tomorrow.

Having only recently completed his own tour of ops, Eric still took a keen interest in how others were doing:

> I spent last evening at a local station to watch the return. I still keep in touch. I haven't got the gen on 61, yet. I saw Bill Hesketh and found him as sociable as ever.

Eric was delighted to be reunited with his former commanding officer from his hectic few weeks in France. Hesketh was now an acting air commodore and in charge of a 'Base', effectively putting him in overall charge of three RAF Bomber Command stations. The Base system was an additional tier of management thought necessary to cope with the ever-expanding force. Eric was also meeting and making new friends:

A THIRD RING, A BABY, A DFC AND A BAR

I've got a very good friend, here, in a Sq/Ldr., who has seen a lot of action in the Battle of B. and in the Desert – ex fighters. He is now coming through on a Bomber tour! He is 36. Another S/Ldr. who is 45 is ex fighters, ex last war, M.C. & bar, D.F.C. & bar, is also going through on a Bomber tour!

The former chap is extremely sociable. Now, here's an interesting comparison. He is 36; I am 24. He owns a farm in Rhodesia and was managing director of a De Havilland Airways Service in S. Africa, before the war. (He is wealthy!) I worked for the L.V. &R. at 22/- per week and had a capital of about £10. He has a total of about 8,000 flying hours. I have a total of 700 flying hours. It is quite possible I shall be instructing him on 4 engine types, if he arrives at Con. Unit when I am through my course! He says he'll give me a job after the war of £500, plus a house and car and 7/6 per hour's instruction I care to give to his patrons! This, of course, was part in fun, but it would be an opening if I wanted to follow it up. He's going down to see his girl-friend, next week, Lady ----, of Mayfair! Makes you think, dunnit! He's a very good type.

While the socialite farm owner remains anonymous, the 'last war' squadron leader to which Eric refers is Vashon Wheeler, a remarkable character who had indeed won the Military Cross (MC) twice and two DFCs, albeit more than twenty years apart. He won his MCs (both in the space of seven days) not in the First World War but rather during the north Russia intervention in 1919, and while still in the Army (The Rifle Brigade). After the conflict, and minus two fingers, Ole Popp, as he was known, emigrated and ran a sheep farm in New Zealand. He subsequently sold the farm and with the proceeds learned to fly, earning a living as an early airline pilot. With the outbreak of the Second World War he lied about his age and joined the RAFVR, winning a DFC as a nightfighter pilot with No. 85 Squadron before taking command of No. 157 Squadron where he was awarded a Bar. Tour expired and given command of a training unit, Wheeler apparently had a one-sided argument with the No. 9 Group Commander and decided to offer his services to Bomber Command instead. A few weeks after meeting Eric, Wheeler was given command of No. 207 Squadron in February but was shot down and killed the following month. He was 46.

On 18 January, three days after writing this letter, Eric received the official notification of the award of a Bar to his own DFC, which this time appeared with an edited citation:

Act. Sqn. Ldr. E. A. Benjamin, D.F.C., RAFVR, No 61 Sqn. – As Captain of aircraft Sqn. Ldr. Benjamin has taken part in many operational sorties, and since being awarded the DFC has attacked some of the enemy's most important targets, including Berlin. An excellent flight commander, his courage and skill in the face of the enemy have been most praiseworthy.

It was a hugely exciting time: in the space of just a few short months Eric had been promoted squadron leader, become a father and been awarded a DFC and Bar and he was still only twenty-four years old. It was somewhat overwhelming:

> There's a year, if you like! A third ring, a baby, a D.F.C. and a Bar! Shakes me!
> But did you know I love you more than ever? Here I am in a new room, but the background is just the same – the usual furniture. There's a table – this table, where I write my letters and watch the clock. But I take more than a single glance at my now familiar little array of pictures. Did you know it's the sweetest thing to look at – you and our little one? If you had paid £10 to have that taken, I would not have regretted a penny of it. I think I've said, before, I think it's perfect.

Now at Swinderby with No. 1660 Conversion Unit (he was formally posted in on 22 January 1944), Eric started to become busy again, being expected to take charge of all night flying activities (as OC Night Flying) every few days. He warned Betty that she might not always be able to speak to him if she rang, and not to be too disappointed. Betty was fretting about the baby while Eric was more concerned about his laundry:

> Haven't you got a little of my laundry? I rather fancy you've one or two towels, a pair of long pants and a pair of pyjamas. Don't worry, though. I've probably got these things right here, in my room, but I can't be bothered to look. That's terrible, isn't it. I know you've my pair of silk pyjamas, though. I expect you're making yourself a pair of knickers out of them. I need another pair – pyjamas, I mean.
> How's my Jeannie, tonight? Such a good little thing, isn't she. The food, here, is very good. Tonight, we had a cold salad – lovely ham. I went to the camp cinema, last night, and saw a ridiculous American Air Force film. It's quite a good cinema – 1/- seats, tell Mam!

At the end of January, Eric was able to get to Teddington for a couple of days' leave. While away, however, there was a terrible accident on the station. A Short Stirling had taken off from Swinderby late one evening for a combined Bullseye and searchlight cooperation exercise with John Greig, an experienced captain, at the controls.[56] For some reason, and possibly because the pilot had become dazzled by the lights, the aircraft dived into the Humber, not far from North Killingholme. Four of the crew were posted as 'missing' and their bodies never recovered: Derek Helsby, who came from Sale near Manchester, Arthur Spence, also from Manchester, Edward Neary from Shrewsbury, and Gwilym Williams, a Welshman from Monmouthshire.

To Eric fell the sombre duty of informing the next of kin, and an eye-opening few days during his unexpected tour:

> You were surprised, of course, to get my wire. Now, here's the story.
>
> I got back with little trouble by 10.30pm last night. This morning (5 February), I was just amusing myself, generally, when the CO said he had a job for me for a few days. There was an accident, while I was away, and four of the bodies have not been recovered, so I've got to go and see the next of kin and explain a few details that could not be put into a letter. The next of kin live at three places – one near here (Manchester), one at Shrewsbury and one at Newport. This means about four days travelling. Hence my 'tour of Wales'.
>
> Well, I dashed off from Swinderby at 2.30, today, and changed at Nottingham, for Manchester. I was dubious about finding a bed when I arrived at 7.30. It was dark and I didn't know the town, of course, but a very charming telephone operator rang all sorts of hotels for me, ending up at a Y.M.C.A. one which had just one bed! I was surprised to find one of these hotels up here. It is a very nice one, too, and was only two minutes from the station. I arrived in time for supper, which was nice, and found the people very courteous. After a meal, I thought I might try the town's beer and see a little of its night life – and I was appalled!
>
> I fought to a bar and had a pint and walked back a ¼ mile to the Y.M.C.A. The whole town, it seems, - the pubs, the cinemas, - the streets – smells of sex. It was light enough to see Americans propped up against women on the pavement and to hear, above the din of the tramways, the intoxicated giggles of sensuous young girls, followed up by some varied assortment of lustful males! The town is full – not simply of people (and I've never seen so many people) – but of sexual intoxication, it seems.
>
> So, tomorrow, in the afternoon (as they might be at Church in the morning) I shall go to the first relatives, who live about fifteen miles out of Manchester. I shall have to stay at this place again tomorrow night and move off to Shrewsbury, Monday morning. I shall be doing nothing but work out train times and wonder where I shall spend each night!
>
> Well, my love, I hope I don't miss any important news from your end. I should think I'll be back at Swinderby on Wednesday, so you

> could write Tuesday. Of course, there's a chance I might be starting my course next Thursday, in which case I'll have to go straight there from Newport, which is quite near. What a to-do!

The course which Eric mentions was at RAF Lulsgate Bottom, near Bristol (now the site of Bristol airport), home to No. 3 Flying Instructors School (3 FIS). He went directly there from Newport to attend a month-long Staff Pilots' Course. He wrote to Betty as soon as he arrived. He had not had time to report the outcome of his tour of the north and was yet to be convinced by his new surroundings. He was, however, keeping an open mind.

> I am writing this in an office, waiting for a call from Swinderby to let them know my 'goings on', so am using the waiting time profitably.
>
> When I say it is cold, it must be, I suppose. I was frozen in my bed, last night. I got here at 10pm and had a fire, but woke up several times in the night, each time bringing my feet higher up the bed! There was only cold water, so I didn't shave and it was bitter, walking down on the aerodrome. I've borrowed a helmet and shall fly to Swinderby in a few days for extra kit.
>
> Don't think I don't like this place, for all that. I shall have a room to myself, tonight, and expect to enjoy the course and the 'atmosphere' in the non-literal sense of the word. My instructor is sick and I don't expect to fly until tomorrow afternoon. Lectures will begin tomorrow morning, and they start very early, 8.30-9.00 or so.

Eric thoroughly enjoyed the course which one contemporary described as the best course he ever attended, military or civilian, in all of his service life. Largely it comprised stooging up and down every day, sometimes three or four times a day, in an Airspeed Oxford or Miles Master advanced trainer, learning the difficult skills of how to teach others to fly. Eric also enjoyed the proximity to home, being able to make a number of journeys by train to Teddington, where Betty was again living with her parents. He wrote to Betty on 12 February while looking proudly at a photograph of his daughter.

> I've been getting along fine with this course. I enjoy every moment of the flying – it's very interesting. I feel I'm a capable instructor already. The instructors here have all the gen, and it's a very good course. The lectures, though, are 'training command' style and are rather a bore and waste of time. The course might be anything from four- to six-weeks. I might be able to get home, next Friday (Thursday night) – Friday being a day off, but there I go – I mustn't tell you these things. I expect to fly to Swinderby tomorrow.

Eric's first doubts about the place had been assuaged and he was enjoying both the training and the social life:

> Thursday night was a 'get together' night for our course and we had beer free. It was a good social evening and I slept well as a result. I am getting used to the place and sleep well now, with bed socks and dressing gown on. I shave overnight, though I generally get a can of hot-water, now, in the morning. I am feeling fit, as a result of all the fresh air walking I get in, - up hill and down dale. This is a lovely spot, very near Cheddar Gorge, which you wouldn't know, but we are near Cheddar Gorge! This is only a matter of about eight miles from Len's place (my nav.). I hope to pop down there. I must write him, tonight.
>
> One of the pilots here is a conjurer – professional. He has baffled us with some simple tricks. He entertained us for quite a time, last night. Also, yesterday teatime, an American Lieutenant gave a talk on their customs and idiosyncrasies. It was a fair insight into American life and ways of living and their apparent wealth. He explained that it is only 5% of Americans you find in pubs throwing away £1 notes. They are the people without dependants or home responsibilities. It was a good talk, and he was very dynamic.

Returning from two days' leave, and back in his 'tin hut', Eric fell ill and reported sick. He had a sore throat and complained of feeling 'mouldy'. By gargling and dosing himself up with aspirin and Codeine, and eating a healthy breakfast, he was soon on the mend and determined to keep flying. While he recognised his wife's concern for his health (including in a letter written on 19 February, exactly one year before his final hurried note to his beloved), Eric was more concerned for Betty's own safety. The Germans had started, albeit rather late in the day, a new 'Blitz'. Known officially as Operation Steinbock and more colloquially as 'the baby Blitz', the Germans amassed almost 500 of their bombers for the offensive which was aimed chiefly at targets in and around London and the South East. It meant a brief return to the regular wail of the air raid siren, and the prickle of fear as residents once again headed for the shelters and the underground. Each time Betty heard the sirens and the frightening drone of German bombers overhead she would hurriedly lift her precious Jeannie from her cot and rush down to the cupboard under the stairs. There she would crouch with her innocent baby in her arms until the 'all clear' siren sounded, and it was finally safe for them to emerge:

> Poor darling and the air raids. It was an early morning one, too, wasn't it? Poor you. I wish I'd been there, so much. What a barrage I must

have missed. I always miss them. It isn't fair! Never mind, perhaps they'll come over next Friday night, when I shall (?) be home, eh?

I have lost my throat – I mean it's gone – it's better. I dosed myself just in time and it was gone, yesterday. The weather is much warmer and still quite good for flying. I did all the night flying we have to do, here, last night – three hours, getting to bed at 1.30. I had a marvellous sleep and got up for a bath at 10. It was a very hot one, too, and I had a good appetite at lunchtime. More flying this afternoon.

Well, we've got exams on Thursday, so I must do a little swotting. I'll write again on Wed., I expect, in the hopes of seeing my Love, on Friday.

Eric was once again able to go home for the weekend of 25/26 February, enjoying more family time with Betty, Jeannie and his in-laws, Mam and Pop. He returned to Bristol via Paddington on a comparatively empty train to find a party in full swing in the Mess. The CO of No. 3 FIS, Jerry Gosnell, had returned from leave, having temporarily handed over command to Mike Stephens, an accomplished fighter pilot, during his absence[57]:

There was a Mess party going on (I forgot to mention it) so I had a look in and sampled the grub and free beer. I've got to pay for it on my Mess Bill, anyway. So I got to bed at 12.30. I slept quite well, too – and that is a good sign, because, d'you know, my dear one, I had most erratic nights when Jerry came over, (except the night before I came home). I didn't tell you. One night last Tuesday, I dreamed I was in the middle of some bombs and, just as one was coming at me, I jumped and hit my head against the hut wall with a bang! I woke up with such a start. (That's not funny!)

Eric also put his head around the door to hear of the adventures of one of his fellow pilots, Douglas Frostick:

I went into the party, primarily, to see S/L Frostick[58] and how he got back in the Oxford. He said he had quite a game and got rather lost, but made it O.K.

All aspects of flying have some elements of danger attached to them and flying instructors' school was no different. Within a few days of Eric's arrival, Flying Officer Rich Rogers and his pupil pilot, Flight Lieutenant Frederick Garvey, were killed when their aircraft crashed on take-off. Garvey was a highly experienced former Pathfinder with both the DSO and DFC. Squadron Leader Frostick wasn't so unlucky, but clearly had an adventure or two worthy of a line shoot in the mess!

After his four-week course at Lulsgate Bottom had finished, and now a qualified flying instructor, Eric returned to RAF Swinderby and No. 1660 CU. He had passed his exams with ease and thoughts increasingly turned to life after the war. While the Second Front had not yet been opened, the tide of the war was clearly turning, and Eric could afford to think of a life without conflict. He could also look forward to his birthday:

> I'm gradually settling down, here, but it is a thankless job. To be honest about it, though it's not a bad job, I don't think I shall really enjoy it. It's certainly better than Scampton. I'm not rushed off my feet, anyway. It's quite fun, really. Don't think I want to get away from here – nothing of the sort.
>
> I've got our young daughter gazing at me while I write. It's rather distracting. She's a wonderful baby you know!
>
> An Air Ministry Order (AMO) has just come out to say that applications for permanent commissions can now be submitted, in view of the possibility of an expanded RAF after the war, though nothing will be decided until after the war. I have put one in. Service required (from date of commission) is 2 ½ years for a rank of F/Lt. For S/Ldr, you have to have held W/Co. for a short period. I must do that! You have got to be under 30.
>
> I had a couple of oranges, yesterday, and have eaten them! I know I should have sent them to you, but don't call me nasty things, eh? Will you remember to get me for my birthday a soap container and a new toilet bag?

Two days later, on 14 March 1944, he wrote again from Swinderby, his letter revealing some of the day-to-day responsibilities of a senior officer in charge of a conversion unit at that time (or at least a flight commander deputising for the OC). He had to arrange not just the usual day- and night-time flying exercises, but also the more advanced Bullseyes for those coming to the end of their training. He had also begun seriously looking for nearby accommodation for all three of them, away from the bombing.

> It's so nice to hear you over the phone. I did enjoy that three minutes. Since then, I have just been down to see how my night flying is going on. I'm not OC, but I take a general interest in 'my boys', you see. I was more than OC last night. I was 'Controller', i.e. Super OC of night flying in all our units. It's quite interesting and it means you are responsible for all cancellations and amendments to night flying and must watch the weather all night and instruct all units accordingly.
>
> When you see the London searchlights playing with our own aircraft,

it may be due to my indirect orders! As controller, I get in touch with the district searchlight people and ask for their co-operation, giving them times, numbers of aircraft, routes, etc. I feel quite important.

I'm glad you were pleased with my fruitless efforts over accommodation. I wish I could have given you glad news. I shan't get a lot of opportunity for scouting around, but something may turn up. What we want, of course, is the 'ideal' – and that is the difficulty. It is not very difficult to find a couple of rooms, but that is useless. For the sake of it, I had a look at some, today, but they would not have suited us even without Jeannie and without being 'fussy'. The old girl was the major snag! There are another couple of rooms becoming available at another place, but they are of no use to us. I also saw a rather nice old girl at a biggish house, but though she was a kindly type similar to Mrs Fisher, she could not help as she was overburdened. All these places were about four miles away – not too badly situated. However, this is all futureless chatter. Perhaps we'll get something in the end, eh?

I'm getting my flight organised. The chaps are quite nice fellows – seven officer instructors, one N.C.O. – and I've organised a 'day-off' roster for them, which they didn't have before. This will depend on the amount of work on hand and I may have to cancel it. One F/O (flying officer) was in my flight in 61. He finished ops last September.

I've clicked for an Investigation into a slight aircraft accident. This is a bind – I have to get written statements from everyone concerned and allocate blame, if any. (Like a Court of Inquiry I did at Bobb. on that road accident.)

The 'slight aircraft accident' was the result of a Stirling being obliged to land with only three engines, the fourth engine having gone u/s. The pilot landed heavily, the aircraft bounced, and on landing a second time the undercarriage collapsed. The pilot, an Australian, and his crew walked away red-faced but otherwise unscathed. Eric dealt with the paperwork.

Despite his ever-growing responsibilities, Eric continued to hunt for suitable accommodation so Betty and the baby could be close by. He was still concerned about the air raids:

Well, darling, you poor thing in the raids, again. I knew they were coming and I only wish I could have got you up here by now. No luck, yet. The only hope is to investigate right in Lincoln. In that case, you would be eight- to nine-miles away and I should have to have an automobile. Whether there is any better chance of a place of the nature we want, inside Lincoln, I don't know. I shall have to get a day off and see, but I am busy, now. I get a number of free evenings, but that's no

A THIRD RING, A BABY, A DFC AND A BAR

time for looking for a place. I can't help thinking that, if I do get a place, the better vehicle to have is a motorbike. There is so much trouble with cars, but not motorbikes and you could get your money back more easily – there's not the deterioration.

I was OC N/F last night, but the weather was kind to me and I was in bed at 11pm.

I rang Len the other day and he asked me to go to a little staff party in Scampton, tonight. The usual problem of transport arose, but I have asked W/Co Baxter (Chief Instructor) to come along and do some 'liaison' in his car! So we're going over there about 8pm. It's about fourteen miles.

I've been getting written evidence, today, on my Investigation. It's very tricky trying to do these odd jobs at the same time as running the flight. I hope to get 'airborne' one day!

On 7 April censorship was imposed on all private correspondence, and the letters to/from Betty dried up. Throughout the summer the Station received a number of 'Darkie' calls from aircraft lost and potentially heading for trouble. The Darkie system was a position fixing procedure using radio transmission so that the pilot of an aircraft who was lost could make contact with the ground and find out where he was. Some of these calls were suspect, however and all personnel were on their guard.

At the beginning of May, Eric took some leave and shortly after they learned that Betty was expecting their second child. Eric's attempts to find somewhere for his family to live now took on a new urgency. His endeavours eventually bore fruit and soon Betty and Jeannie had moved up to the outskirts of Lincoln near the airbase. They were at last able to spend time enjoying family life together. Betty wrote in her memoir:

> He found digs for me in Lincoln near the aerodrome and we lived a 'normal' married life for a while. Took Jeannie in carry cot to mess parties. Then we were somewhat dismayed to find I was pregnant again, but soon adjusted.

On 6 June 1944, the Allies opened the long-awaited Second Front, accelerating the countdown to ultimate victory. It took some time for the beachhead to become established and for the land forces to break out of Normandy, but as they did the intensity of bombing operations grew significantly. A few months earlier, Harris had authorised a significant change in Bomber Command's organisation and structure. Since August 1942, every major attack on the enemy had been led by aircraft from Pathfinder Force, a force that was given Group status (as No. 8 Group) in

January 1943. The AOC No. 8 Group, Donald Bennett, had very definite views on how ground targets should be identified and marked, and was a particular advocate of marking from height. Sir Ralph Cochrane, Bennett's opposite number at No. 5 Group, had similarly firm views that more accurate bombing results could be achieved by marking at lower levels. After a particularly tetchy exchange involving Bennett, Cochrane and Sir Arthur Harris after a series of poor results over Berlin, Harris ordered Bennett to return the No. 5 Group Squadrons that had been loaned to him on the formation of PFF and subsequently allowed Cochrane to experiment with his own brand of 'pathfinding'. The '5 Group Method' used Mosquitoes to mark at very low level in a gliding attack, where they could visually identify the target once it had been illuminated by an allocated 'Flare Force'. While the Mosquito was the primary aircraft used for such a purpose, No. 5 Group also experimented with the Mustang (flown successfully by one of the greater bomber pilots of all time, Leonard Cheshire) and even the Lockheed Lightning with its distinctive twin-boom tail.

Within No. 8 Group, certain outstanding aircraft captains on each squadron were designated as raid controllers, the so-called 'Master Bombers'. A 'Master' and a 'Deputy' would be present in each case, to issue instructions to their own pathfinding aircraft and Main Force crews as to where they should drop their bombs to ensure the accuracy and success of their attack. Within No. 5 Group they took a different approach, effectively creating a 'pool' of Master Bombers (often referred to as Master Controllers in 5 Group-speak) concentrated at a Base (a unit of command between a station and a Group) and borrowing aircraft from one of their Base squadrons. In the case of No. 54 Base, for example, which covered the three airfields of RAF Coningsby, RAF Woodhall Spa and RAF Metheringham, Master Controllers had access to the Mosquitoes of No. 627 Squadron at Woodhall Spa.

Keeping the talent all in one place had many practical advantages. It allowed experienced men to learn from each other. The schooling of controllers covered many aspects: radio procedures; codes; enemy countermeasures; low-level marking; and, of course, total mastery of the aircraft they flew. Anyone wanting to be considered for joining the No. 5 Group marking team had to first complete and pass a short conversion course at the PFF Mosquito Conversion Unit at RAF Warboys. Famously, and for reasons never quite explained or understood before or since, the most revered of all wartime bomber pilots, Guy Gibson, managed to find his way into leading a Main Force raid as a Master Controller without any such training, and with only a handful of hours on a Mosquito. Marking involved a gliding attack from around 3,000ft down to 600ft followed by a climb out with such vigour that the navigator could sometimes black out.

The wing loading of a Mosquito was very high and upon pulling out of a dive the aircraft could continue to sink a few hundred feet before she would resume level flight and climb again. This took serious practice, and experience was key. Gibson was lost on his one and only 'pathfinding' operation on the night of 19 September 1944, and it is generally accepted that lack of experience on type and using this specific technique may have played a role.

A few weeks after Gibson's death, having had his application to join the élite band of Master Bombers accepted, Eric arrived at No. 54 Base, along with another pilot, Dennis Stubbs, to make up for Gibson's loss. Both were formally posted for Master Bomber duties, the post warranting the rank of wing commander. For now, however, the men retained their acting squadron leader status.

Within a few days, Eric and Dennis were despatched to RAF Warboys for further instruction[59] and training on the aircraft they would fly on operations, much to the consternation of Eric's wife who was now almost six-months pregnant:

> Eric's posted, isn't it awful? He's going on Mosquitos.

A famous photo of No. 5 Group Master Bombers and groundcrew including John Woodroffe (far right). Eric is third from right.

Chapter Six

Master Bomber

Eric arrived at No. 54 Base from No. 1660 CU on 26 October 1944, his posting coinciding with something of a changing of the guard. Alfred 'Bobby' Sharp, the long-serving and somewhat controversial Base Commander, was promoted air vice marshal to take on a new post with the air force in south east Asia. His place was taken by Harry Satterly, a former Halton Apprentice who had risen through the ranks to command No. 83 Squadron early in the war. More recently he'd been No. 5 Group Senior Air Staff Officer (SASO)[60].

If the Pathfinders were the élite, then the Master Bombers can be considered the élite of the élite, and the men understandably keen to prove their skills. And if a man can be judged by the company he keeps, then Eric was one of the most sought-after men in No. 5 Group, if not the whole of Bomber Command.

Eric arrived at RAF Coningsby to find a small cadre of men of equal or more senior rank proudly sporting the golden eagle, the mark of a Pathfinder, beneath their flying 'wings' and medal ribbons,. The eagle was not awarded on joining PFF; it had to be earned and officially granted by an awarding committee, and all of Eric's contemporaries had earned theirs several times over.

First among them, perhaps, was a jovial wing commander who introduced himself as John Woodroffe. Tall, with sharp features and a proud nose, John was six years older than Eric, and a regular officer as opposed to a VR. John had learned to fly in 1938, serving in the Middle East and India before returning to the UK and joining Main Force. He had more than forty operations to his name, many as a Master Bomber. He also introduced himself as the Base Training Officer for good measure, responsible for the technical efficiency of the squadrons under Base control.

Shortly before Eric's arrival, on the night of 6/7 October, Woodroffe had been controlling a raid on Bremen when he was coned and intercepted by an enemy nightfighter, only narrowly escaping with his life. He'd had a similarly hairy trip in the second week of November, flak taking out his air speed indicator and damaging the hydraulics, and obliged to crash land at an emergency airfield operated by Coastal Command[61]. On recommending Woodroffe for a DSO in December 1944, Cochrane described him as being so accomplished at his job that any operation for which he was appointed Master Bomber 'was bound to succeed.'

Alongside Woodroffe was another wing commander, Maurice Smith, who'd learned to fly as an eighteen-year-old with the Oxford University Air Squadron in 1934, while studying at Wadham College. He'd also trained as an engineer with the Rolls Royce apprentice school in Derby before joining the editorial team at *Flight* magazine in 1936, where his practical flying skills and technical knowledge of engines and associated systems were much valued by editors and readers alike. He spent much of the early war as an instructor in Canada, adding significantly to his flying hours, before returning to the UK and a tour with No. 619 Squadron Main Force. His skills as a pilot, and as an outstanding navigator, were soon realised and he was invited to join Pathfinder Force. Like Woodroffe, he already had around forty operations to his name.

George Petty, the third man to have three thick rings on his sleeve, had also learned to fly before the war. He'd served with No. 76 Squadron out of RAF Finningley flying the Vickers Wellesley, famous for achieving a series of long-range flying records, before converting to the Hampden and moving to No. 83 Squadron. It was in a Hampden that he flew his first tour and was awarded the DFC. The diagonal white and purple striped ribbon of the DFC on his tunic was complemented by the distinctive colours of the DSO, awarded for a further tour of operations as a flight commander with No. 207 Squadron on Lancasters, by which time he was an acting squadron leader. A slight man with an obligatory RAF moustache, George was seldom seen without a cigarette in his hand.

Completing the ensemble was Dennis Stubbs, the man with whom Eric had arrived. Prematurely balding, Stubbs, who similarly sported a classic handlebar moustache, was also awaiting his promotion to wing commander. Stubbs had spent the early part of the war on fighters with Nos 601 and 238 Squadrons in the winter of 1940, having been hospitalised in the summer after an accident. He then became an instructor and spent more than two years training novice aircrew how to master their craft over the vast South African veldt. Returning to the UK he converted to Lancasters and joined No. 9 Squadron as OC A Flight before becoming OC B Flight at No. 50 Squadron in the summer of 1944.

Beneath his pilot's wings was the ribbon of the DFC awarded to him the month prior to joining Pathfinders in October 1944 for leading a successful raid on the oil storage tanks at La Pallice by the historic town of La Rochelle on the west coast of France. Stubbs had to fight his way through atrocious weather and heavy and accurate fire from the enemy defences to make good his attack and was credited for his 'high standard of leadership, courage and unswerving devotion to duty.'[62]

To Dennis Stubbs, a married man, the war was intensely personal. He was one of five brothers who served in the RAF, one of whom, Cecil, was killed when his No. 44 Squadron Hampden was blown out of the sky on 21 October 1940 when navigating his aircraft to Berlin. Another brother, Robert, was shot down while serving with No. 158 Squadron on 24 May 1944. He was the rear gunner in a Halifax and survived but was traumatised by the experience and his subsequent incarceration in a PoW camp. A third brother, Stanley, lost an eye.[63]

Among this exalted company, Eric patiently waited his turn. As a Mosquito pilot he was now flying arguably the finest all-round fighting aircraft of the war, a wooden miracle that could fly high and fight hard in multiple roles, armed and unarmed, over land or sea. Having spent the past few months flying doughty but unimpressive Oxfords and catching the odd trip in a battered Stirling whilst at Swinderby, to be at the controls of a Mosquito was a thrill, and Eric was eager to prove his mettle. He was also now part of a team of two, as opposed to seven, with Jack Heath, a recently commissioned former NCO in the navigator's seat.

Jack Heath was absolutely no stranger to bomber operations. A Lancashire lad from the pretty parish of Mellor, a few miles to the west of Blackburn, Jack was a proven survivor whose operational career in Main Force had largely mirrored that of his captain's. Qualifying as an observer, after completing his training at No. 1654 HCU, he'd been posted with his captain, 'Jimmy' Wilkie, and crew to No. 50 Squadron in March 1943, and by the early summer they had completed their first dozen trips, mostly to the Ruhr. Then came the dramatic night of June 28/29 when they were briefed to attack Cologne. Over the target area, their Lancaster was hit by flak, a shell exploding in close proximity to the aircraft, shattering the windscreen around the cockpit area, causing Jimmy to cry out in alarm and pain as flying splinters stung his face and rendered him temporarily blind. The pilot was not the only one hurt: the air bomber was also wounded in the arm in three places, and Jack hit in the shoulder. A second navigator had shrapnel in his leg, while further down the aircraft, the mid-upper gunner was considering the loss of one of his fingers.

Jimmy stayed at the controls, despite the pain and the panic welling up inside him through loss of sight, while his flight engineer and air bomber did what they could to help guide their captain through the defences and successfully complete the bombing run. Flying almost entirely by feel and touch, and managing to avoid the worst of the searchlights and the flak, Jimmy made it clear of the target area while Jack gave him a course to steer for home. Although still in considerable discomfort, vision began clearing in one eye, enough for pilot, crew and aircraft to make it safely back to Britain. Not surprisingly, Jimmy Wilkie was awarded the Conspicuous Gallantry Medal (CGM) for his bravery, beaten only by the Victoria Cross and George Cross in the hierarchy of gallantry awards, and three other members of the crew, the air bomber (Edward Hearn), flight engineer (Stanley Wilkinson) and mid upper gunner (Frank Pointon), were also decorated. Jack might have considered himself unlucky that he too was not recognised for his efforts, in navigating their aircraft home despite his wounds. (Wilkie returned to operations in August and was killed on the night of 4/5 October 1943 over Frankfurt, along with his flight engineer.)

Jack's wounds took time to heal, and by the time he was ready to fly again he was allocated to a different captain, Harry Shortt, a Canadian with the DFC, a flight lieutenant and deputy flight commander, and a most accomplished captain of aircraft. Even the best captains and navigators could sometimes be caught out, however, and on the night of 27/28 September, returning from Hanover, the crew became lost in bad weather. Attempting to land at RAF Lissett in the East Riding of Yorkshire, some sixty miles north of their own base at RAF Skellingthorpe, Harry overshot the runway, unaware of a vicious cross wind, and the aircraft was badly damaged. Happily, there was no damage to the crew who returned to the squadron the next day, none the worse for their endeavours.

The tour Jack completed was typical of those, like Eric, who flew in some of Arthur Harris' major 'battles' in 1943/early 1944, when the German defences were at their peak. On the night of 20/21 October, on a long slog to Leipzig in the east, Jack's Lancaster was hit several times over the target, creating holes in the fuselage and flaps. As the pilot headed for home, they were then attacked by a twin-engine nightfighter that failed to get the better of the air gunners who between them fired off more than a 1,000 rounds as the skipper gently corkscrewed to avoid the incoming attacks. The rear gunner kept firing until a ball of fire erupted in the sky and the fighter was deemed probably destroyed. The combat had consumed more fuel than was safe, given the distance left to travel, and it was a much-relieved crew who landed at RAF Foulsham in Norfolk after a trip of more than nine and a half hours with the last few litres of petrol left in the tanks.

Commissioned at the end of 1943, Jack completed his tour in late January, his last three trips being to the German capital, and surviving one more encounter with an enemy fighter. Tour expired, he was awarded a well-earned DFM on 18 January 1944, and rested at a Lancaster Finishing School. Hankering for a return to operations, he was delighted to team up

MASTER BOMBER 91

with Eric to start a new tour.

The new team took the Deputy's role for an attack on Heilbronn on 4/5 December which Eric alludes to in a letter to Betty on the evening of his return. He was also due to be operating again that same night, but the operation was called off. Eric joked about it in his next letter home:

> I was so pleased to hear your sweet voice tonight. I simply wanted – just wanted you to ring and I was waiting shortly before 7. I do love you. He!
>
> It was extraordinarily fortunate, too, because I was to have been over the 'Greater Reich' about that time, but it was cancelled. I didn't tell them you were going to ring – it must have been cancelled for some other reason! As I said, I was on the night before and to be honest I wasn't really the Master Bomber – I couldn't go on explaining over the phone – I was a deputy, but tonight I was to have been in 'supreme control'.

While there was drama in the air, there was also drama on the ground. Eric had contrived one evening to run over a cat in the blackout, but now had gone one worse and run over a dog:

> A wretched nuisance of a thing happened, tonight. You remember the cat I 'bumped off'. Well I had the same misfortune in the dark, tonight, only it was a dog. Awful nuisance, as a dog has to be reported to the police and I went and saw the local bobby and took the dog to the owner – a local farmer. He was quite understanding and there was no bother, but it was just a nuisance.

Eric's disappointment at not being the Master Bomber was short-lived. The following evening, 6/7 December 1944, he and Jack received the exciting news they had been waiting for. While the five other Main Force Groups of Bomber Command split their forces to attack oil targets at Leuna and the railway yards at Osnabruck, Cochrane's 'Independent Air Force' as it was disparagingly known in certain circles, was being allotted the target of Giessen, some thirty-five miles to the North of Frankfurt. Eric was appointed Master Controller.

By this stage there was an established No. 5 Group routine for such attacks. Pathfinder Mosquito crews from No. 627 Squadron were allotted specific tasks, divided between 'markers' and 'windfinders'. Markers were responsible for finding and marking the target, illuminated by the 'Flare Force' of Lancasters from either Nos 83 or 97 Squadrons, and dropping Target Indicators (TIs) where they perceived the aiming point to be. The Master Controller (Eric) would then assess the accuracy of the markers, and either call for more TIs to be dropped, the initial TIs to be backed-up, or for Main Force to come in and bomb. Windfinders (led by a 'Breeze Leader') supported the attack by establishing the wind speed and direction, at the attack height in the target area, so that the data could be fed into the bombsight mechanisms of the Main Force aircraft.

(Bill Burke, a 20-year old No. 627 Squadron Nav recalls: 'One flew to a pre-determined point close to the target, a marker was put down on the ground, and using the Mosquito's bomb sight the navigator guided the pilot over the marker noting the precise time and air position. By repeating the operation three or four minutes later the navigator could make the required wind calculations. Three aircraft were used and by Radio Transmitter (R/T) the three navigators' assessments could be broadcast, with one navigator determining the mean. This would be relayed to the 'heavies' which would be closing in on the target. To be frank, I hated the job!')[64]

The attack on Giessen involved a force of 255 heavy bombers (all Lancasters) and nine Mosquitoes, the force being split into two: 168 aircraft allocated to the town centre and 87 to the railway yards. It was not uncommon to have two aiming points, but it certainly added a complication, and to that end Eric was delighted with the choice of Deputy. Ronnie Churcher, a Flight Commander on 627, was one of the most experienced Mosquito pilots with two tours behind him. He'd been the Deputy on the night that Guy Gibson had been lost and was considered a 'practised hand'.[65]

With the marshalling yards some one-and-a-half miles south of the town, marking was a challenge. The solution was to select a common marking point to the south of the yards and provide the marshalling yard force with two false wind vectors calculated such that the bombs would explode in the centre of the target. The force allocated to the town centre was to carry out a normal overshoot procedure (i.e flying beyond the aiming point for a few brief seconds before dropping their bombs) on a common heading.

Apart from one of the Mosquitoes being obliged to return early, the attack went like clockwork. The target was well illuminated by the Pathfinder Lancasters and the Mosquitoes had little trouble in identifying and marking the target or backing up the first TIs. While the windfinders didn't have their best day, Main Force bombed accurately and on time. The post-raid analysis[66] suggested that a heavy concentration of bombs fell on the yards, destroying the round houses and causing considerable damage to rolling stock and various important bridges that served the depot. The town itself was also severely hit, the main city area to the north receiving particular attention. A rubber factory, an arsenal, gas and waterworks, and a power station were known to be destroyed or believed put out of action.

Perhaps somewhat surprisingly, Eric makes no mention of the operation, even in passing, in any of his letters home. Betty was in the last stage of pregnancy, and he doubtless did not want to alarm her any more than necessary. Christmas was fast approaching, and with Betty in the last few weeks of her pregnancy, Eric was desperate to spend it with his wife and Jeannie. It appears his application for Leave looked promising, and on the late evening of Tuesday 12 December, he penned the following letter home:

> I got your call tonight, as usual. How lucky we are. It's so nice. Yes, and I let the secret out of the bag about next Monday! It's pretty certain, angel, and in that case, you'll probably only get one more letter before then. I'm thrilled to bits! It's rather impossible to give you a time of arrival, but it won't be very early – tea time. But you mustn't get excited – you're expectant!
>
> Yes, I played football, yesterday, and I'm stiff as can be, today. Shall be playing again tomorrow, if there's no war.
>
> Well, dear, I had to write you a short line, but I must get some sleep in now – I dozed off in the Mess this evening. I was late (1.30am) last night! There was a small WAAF party. Quite nice and a bit crowded in their small mess.
>
> Goodnight then, Angel.
>
> Love to all. Hope you've got some turkeys & things.

Two days later, on the night of 14 December, he wrote to Betty again, excited by the prospect of Leave, and this time making an oblique reference to his recent endeavours:

> Just a short one, hoping I shall be with – hoping very much I shall be with you very soon after you receive this. As far as I can see, nothing should prevent me going on leave on Monday. It's so much to look forward to, isn't it. This last week is a terrific drag, but it's Friday, tomorrow, and there's only the week-end, then.
>
> Well, dear, I was out on a rather long 'op', last night, but I can't discuss it. I didn't get a proper sleep and I'm turning in for a good night's rest, now.

The 'long op' to which Eric refers was indeed a marathon for the Mosquito crews taking part.

Since the very early days of the bombing war, the Royal Navy had exerted its influence as the Senior Service to ensure some of Bomber Command's resources were given over to attacking German naval vessels. Besides the ubiquitous U-Boat threat, they feared the havoc a German surface raider might cause if let loose in the Atlantic, with some justification.

It prompted a series of raids on the battleships *Scharnhorst* and the *Gneisenau*, for example, as they sheltered in La Pallice. After the infamous Channel Dash incident, in which the two ships, in the company of the heavy cruiser *Prinz Eugen*, thumbed their noses at both the RN and the RAF and made good their escape from France to safe havens in Germany, the ships continued to present a very real danger. Their mere presence was enough to keep a significant number of RN vessels tied down and permanently on station, ships that were urgently needed elsewhere.

By the end of 1944, however, this threat had all but disappeared. *Gneisenau* went into dry dock and never came out; *Scharnhorst* was sunk in the Battle of the North Cape in December 1943; and *Prinz Eugen* was torpedoed and never quite the same again. Even the biggest of big beasts, the *Tirpitz*, the sister ship to the more famous *Bismarck* which had been lost in 1941, was no more. She had become almost an obsession with naval and air force commanders alike and was now lying capsized in the cold waters of a Norwegian Fiord, the result of a final attack by RAF Lancasters, the day after Eric's return from Warboys, using 12,000lb 'Tallboy' bombs.

Smaller ships, however, remained. The light cruiser *Emden*, for example, was still a nuisance, as was the *Koln*, both armed with 15cm guns. *Emden* had been the subject of aerial attacks from the very start of the war. On 4 September 1939, while tied up at Wilhelmshaven having returned from laying a defensive minefield, she'd been attacked by a force of ten Bristol Blenheims, five of which were shot down, one crashing into the ship and killing or injuring 29 sailors.[67] (By some unusual quirk, the name of the pilot who died in the crash was Emden). She was quickly repaired and soon in action, however, supporting the German invasion of Norway and later being assigned to the Baltic Fleet for the attack on Russia.

The *Koln*, like the *Emden*, had earned her spurs early in the war, and taken part in a series of patrols, one in the company of the heavy cruisers *Admiral Scheer* (sunk by British bombers four weeks before the end of hostilities) and *Admiral Hipper* (damaged beyond repair by Allied bombing on 3 May 1945) to intercept Convoy PQ18. By the summer of 1944, however, both the *Emden* and the *Koln* were little more than glorified escort vessels for German merchant ships and laying defensive minefields in the Skagerrak. British Intelligence located them, skulking in the Oslofjord, an inlet in the south east of Norway. The order was given for their destruction.

By this stage of the war, the RAF had an established routine for attacking targets so far north. Bombers would fly from their home bases and disperse to RAF stations in Scotland. There they would refuel, prior to making the direct flight over the North Sea to Norway, more than 450 miles. A small force of Lancasters was chosen for the attack exclusively taken from No. 54 Base operating as a self-contained bomber unit for the very first time. They would be led by a contingent of seven Mosquitoes from No. 627, dispersed to RAF Peterhead. Two Pathfinder squadrons, No. 83 (dispersed to RAF Tain) and No. 97 (dispersed to RAF Milltown) would provide target illumination and additional marking to enable the master bomber to guide twenty Lancasters from No. 106 Squadron (dispersed to RAF Kinloss) onto the target, acting as the 'Main Force'.

Eric was told in the morning that he was to be the controller for the raid, with Ronnie Churcher as his Deputy, and immediately set about making plans and securing himself an aircraft. Shortly after 13.00hrs, John Woodroffe set off in a Spitfire to oversee arrangements at RAF Peterhead for the arriving Mosquitoes and to ensure sufficient quantities of 100 octane fuel and oil were available. Eric took off an hour later.

The crews were briefed in the early afternoon and the first Lancasters set off from their dispersed stations shortly after 15.00hrs. The Mosquitoes, lighter and faster, took off an hour and a half later, all except one which had gone u/s. The importance of the target is perhaps evidenced by the seniority of the men taking part. Besides Eric and Ronnie Churcher, the OC No. 627 Squadron, George Curry, was also flying, while in the 'heavies' the OCs of both No. 83 Squadron (John Ingham) and No. 97 Squadron (Peter Johnson) had also chosen to go. Squadron commanders were limited in the number of operations they were allowed to fly every month and must have considered the raid one not to be missed.

The Lancasters had a long but uneventful outward leg, helped by route markers dropped by designated Pathfinder aircraft along the way. As they approached the target, aircraft from Nos 83 and 97 Squadrons dropped Green proximity markers blindly using H2S, after which Ronnie Churcher dropped his Red TIs and ordered Marker 4 (Arthur Wimsett) to back them up. Circling overhead, Eric assessed the markers as having slightly overshot the target, but probably only by 100 yards or so, and called for illumination. The first flares went down on time, and Eric called for more flares to be dropped, slightly to the west of where the TIs were still burning in the gloom. Eric was happy; he could clearly see the two ships in the light of the flares and calmly issued his instructions to 'come in and bomb'.

The aircraft that were on time were the most fortunate as the first of the 1000-pounders went down and straddled the ships below. Several near misses were recorded as bombs exploded in the icy fjord, the effect of the churned water easily observed from the aircraft above. Somewhat disobligingly, however, the ships began making smoke and steaming northwards, which meant they were no longer illuminated and almost impossible to spot. Many of the bomb aimers were unable to see either ship, and those who were lucky to catch a glimpse of anything were unsure as to its identity. Eric called for more flares a full ten minutes after the raid had begun and urged the tiny force to continue their attack. His instructions, however, caused some confusion among those who still had bombs left in their bomb bays (Pathfinder aircraft carried bombs as well as flares and/or TIs), not helped by the fact that the ships were now no longer in their briefed position.

Not wanting to waste the effort, Eric identified what looked like a large merchant vessel in the harbour and asked for the last few bombs to be aimed in its direction. With the last of the flares now used up, and little hope of hitting a moving target, even if they could see it, he ordered the crews to return home. While none of the aircraft was lost in the raid, one Lancaster from 106 overshot the runway landing at RAF Kinloss, while another was diverted to RAF Lossiemouth to land on three engines. At 21.59, all aircraft were recorded as having returned safely and at 00.45, in the small hours of the morning, the Coningsby Operations Room Log noted that a message had been received from No. 83 Squadron at RAF Tain that all of its crews had been interrogated except one who had gone to bed![68] (A post raid assessment suggested that none of the ships targeted had been hit, but in fact several near-misses on the *Koln* caused damage to her propulsion system.)

A few days after returning to RAF Coningsby and writing to Betty, Eric went home on leave on what was to be his last Christmas with his wife and family. The days passed too quickly, and soon Eric was journeying back to Coningsby, at the wheel of his own car. He wrote as soon as he arrived back on the evening of Wednesday, 27 December:

> Well, Angel, I hope you are getting to bed about now, as I am. I enjoyed my leave so much and we must be thankful. It was so nice.
>
> The journey was quite a good one. I took the different route through Brentford and knocked four miles off the journey. The fog was not bad and got better out of London. The roads, though, got worse towards Peterborough and it was quite dangerous as they were icy. I had to drive below 40 mph. and as a result I didn't get back until nearly 6-00, but it was no trouble in the dark, as there was a full moon and the snowy white helped considerably. There was no icing on the windscreen. I enjoyed the sandwiches and the drink was very hot – too hot. I gave an airman a lift from Hendon to Huntingdon, and three Americans a short lift. So it wasn't a bad journey and it was only my feet that got cold.
>
> It has been very cold up here and very foggy. Things have been pretty quiet. I went to the Mess for some supper and had a drink with the local padré (civvy). In fact, it was a little interesting chat I had with him – he was Lincoln prison chaplain for nine years.

So, my dear, I must bath and get to bed. I am with you so much, my love – do look after yourself and let me know how things are going.

'Things have been pretty quiet' is perhaps not wholly accurate. While Eric was away, his fellow Controllers had been busy on consecutive nights: Dennis Stubbs led a largely successful attack on Munich, while John Woodroffe attacked the Polish port of Gydnia, in what contemporary records describe as being 'the main base for what remains of the elusive German fleet' as well as 'a large concentration of U-boats'. Two nights later (21/22 December), Woodroffe was again in action leading an attack on the synthetic oil refinery at Politz, another long slog to the east.

The failure to sink the *Koln* and the *Emden* at the first time of asking obliged No. 5 Group to try again on the night of 28/29 December. On this occasion Eric was to share the controller duties with George Petty, and because of the bright moon, they decided to dispense with flare illumination. Instead, the marker force would drop Wanganui flares (i.e sky markers) and flame floats (marine markers that illuminated a surrounding area of water). Preparations for the attack followed a similar pattern as before, with a few significant variations. Eric was to fly direct to the target from RAF Coningsby and only land at RAF Peterhead if short of fuel or directed to do so by signal. Aside from Eric's Mosquito, it was also to be an all-Lancaster affair and No. 627 Squadron was stood down. The force was also split into two: the larger force was to go for the *Koln*, lying in waters to the west; the smaller force to bomb any shipping to the east.

Much like the previous raid, it enjoyed little success. The weather was clear and there was good visibility which allowed some ships to be seen and bombed but with little discernible result. Flak from the ships in the harbour and the harbour town of Horten itself also caused problems, and at least one of the Lancasters sustained flak damage, but other than that there was little to report. Post raid interrogations and analysis suggested that one large merchant vessel off Moss, on the eastern shore of the Oslofjord, may have been hit, but little else. Eric did not get back to Base until 02.24hrs and immediately 'phoned the AOC to give his report. He finally climbed into bed, exhausted, two hours later.

The arduous six-hour trip took its toll physically on the men taking part, not least Eric's navigator, Jack Heath, who reported sick the following day. Eric makes mention of the raid, and his navigator's troubles, in a letter home on 29th:

Well, I couldn't have spoken a truer word when I said to Pop, on Wednesday, that I should be on ops on Thursday night. For I was. It has just been announced on the wireless that Lancasters bombed shipping in Oslo Fiord (sic), Norway, last night. It was a beautiful trip – full moon, little cloud and lots of snow on the mountains of Norway. It was a very long trip, though, and it was nice to get to bed at 4.30 this morning. I got up for lunch and this afternoon I went down to the local garage to fix up one or two things. They produced a new cap for the petrol tank, saying I was very lucky as they're hard to get. Only 1/3. Tell Pop. I'm going to try to get my new tyres fixed on Monday.

What d'you think! We've got mice in our room in the Mess! They've been attracted by the food parcel sent to an Australian in the room. He had one running over his feet the other night in bed! Last night, I fancied one was tickling my head!

My poor old Navigator came back with a cold and was sick on the trip, - so he wasn't feeling so bright. He's a lot better today.

I said I would leave something behind! Did you find my pipe and pouch in the green coat? I can't smoke your Christmas present until I get it! And I'm spending money on cigarettes, meantime, so you'd better send it!

More money! – As there's such a shortage of batmen, we're to get 2/- a day servant allowance. The batmen or women will only then be expected to make beds and press suits occasionally. I expect I'll still get boots and buttons cleaned, though. Another 14/- a week isn't to be sniffed at. As it's an 'allowance', it's free from income tax, too!

Well, Angel, I'm settling down again, now. The first day was as lousy as ever it was on return from leave, but having to do an op right away soon got me back in to the run of things. I hope you are back in your routine.

Is it Monday, today? Then it's pinch-punch, whatsit! Boo! And many of 'em in 1945. Compliments of the season and New Year greetings to my mother & father-in-law!

The New Year of 1945 dawned, and Eric had plenty to be grateful for. Although not yet a wing commander, he had a promotion to look forward to as well as a new baby. Betty had already chosen the name Sally if it turned out to be a girl and John if it was a boy. Eric's mind was very much on babies. His sister Queenie had already had two children by then, both of them girls (Sylvia and Joan) but Eric and his sister had not been in regular contact since her banishment from the family many years previously. His next letter home on 1 January made no mention of the war, Eric appearing more concerned about having to clean his own buttons and chop his own wood for the stove. He was happy, however, to be reunited with his pipe, and solve a mystery regarding a Christmas Card signed 'Jack':

Happy New Year.

I'm puffing away at my old pipe which arrived today, thank you very much. The tobacco you gave me is not too bad.

They really mean not to clean our boots & buttons, now. As from today, we've really got to clean our own! I shall have to get some brushes & polish, quickly! It's a bit much, isn't it!

It was nice to hear from you this morning and specially that Sally is sitting the right way round. I hope your bum is getting better. Good thing you caught that 'flu, in time, - or should I say 'didn't catch it'!

Yes, Queenie has had one baby, I think.

I'm going strong at wood-chopping. I did a lot, tonight. It's a bit warmer, today.

I think I shall be free to get your phone call tomorrow night. We've been very busy these last few days, but I've only done the one. I hope you get through easily, love. Don't catch cold!

There was a little drinking last night to celebrate, but I turned in before 10 as I had started celebrating a bit early and was quite dizzy!

Well, Angel, that's all for now.

P.S. That card from JACK was my navigator!! - He asked me if I got it and it suddenly came to me!

On the evening of Tuesday 3 January, Betty, now eight months pregnant, wrapped herself up warmly and walked to the red public telephone box up the road to 'phone her husband as she had been doing at least once a week whenever he was away. This evening however, despite many attempts, she was unable to get through. After dialling the number over and over again she eventually gave up and walked sadly back home in the cold, feeling very frustrated and miserable. She was worried, and knew that Eric would be worried too. He wrote on the Wednesday:

Poor old me – or is it poor old you? I wonder why I haven't had your phone call – you're not ill are you angel? I had a letter this morning saying you were looking forward to phoning Tuesday, so I can't make out what's wrong. I know I've said don't wait in a phone box if it's cold and if you're not feeling up to the mark, but you don't take any notice of that, usually. I just don't know what to think. The lines could have been congested, but it's been for two nights. I can only wait for a letter. It would be silly to get worried before I hear something. So I must just wait. I've been free both evenings, too. Ah well, never mind, eh?

What a little devil young Jeannie was the other night. But it must have been lovely, really. I would have loved to have had her in bed with me! I wonder if my compilation of Jeannie's vocabulary amused you. I think I got all her words, didn't I? Made me laugh as I wrote them down.

I greased & washed my car last night. I've got 2 new tyres, now. They look marvellous. They cost £4:17:0, but I shall get a few shillings allowed on the old ones.

Well, my dearest, let me have some news. I'm so anxious.

Two days later Eric stopped worrying:

It was so nice to get two letters this morning. How relieved I was to find it was just that you couldn't get through on the phone. I'm as bad as you – imagining things! You were quite right, darling, not to wait, standing in the phone box. It can do you no good to stand about at this stage. I'm so glad you didn't.

I'm glad you were tickled by my list of Jeannie's words. I had no idea Jeannie would be so amused, as well! I wish I could have seen her.

In the same letter, Eric allowed himself to say a little of his work:

I got airborne in a Lanc today, for a change. Haven't done much flying since the day after I got back. There have been the usual 'flaps' and a few ops, but I've not been required. I've been doing a lot of 'bumf' work.

Life at RAF Coningsby during the first part of this year was becoming a little humdrum. The Tuesday phone calls were the highlight of the week.

There's very little news this time, but it's a line. I've just been 'having a do'. I got out the old polish and things, cleaned three pairs of shoes, made up my laundry for tomorrow and cleaned my pipe! But those pipe-cleaners are useless! They just won't work – they won't go into the pipe and, anyway, the cotton on them just comes off as you force them into the pipe. However, I managed it.

I had a quiet evening, yesterday. We had some scallops for supper – lovely! By the way, you were saying you couldn't get fish when I was home. For the first week I got back, I think we had fish five times! Poor civvies! Well, that's enough on food.

The Camp Cinema is showing 'Madame Curie' tonight. I think I'll go. Looking forward to Tuesday. I bet I'll be 'working'!

On Thursday 11 January Eric went to an ENSA (Entertainments National Service Association) show. This was the organisation set up to provide entertainment for the armed forces. ENSA shows could be somewhat hit and miss affairs, resulting in the Association being retitled 'Every Night Something Awful'. They were still popular, however, and a break from the usual routine:

> I'm going to an ENSA show tonight, so have to hurry this a bit. I don't know what sort of show it is, but I haven't been to an ENSA for years. I went to the pictures last night! 'In Our Time'. I thought I had seen it and I had! I think we saw it together, didn't we?
> Yes, the snow is still with us and still coming. I'm quite an 'office worker' these days. Flying seems to be out of the picture, altogether. I rang Len up, today, just to see how he was getting along. He's quite fit and has done 16 on his second tour.
> By the way, 'Madame Curie' was a dull bind of a picture.
> Yes, it is lovely to hear you every week, my love. It does bring us together. I'm glad you mentioned this in your letter. It was nice.
> What a pity about the pram. Still, you'll find one – there's plenty of time. You went to the doc, today, I suppose. I hope you're quite fit, love. Don't slip over this icy weather. How does Jeannie like the snow? Has she been playing snowballs? I'd like to play snowballs with her. Does she say 'snow'? I'd love to hear her say 'darling'.

A few days later, on the night of Saturday 13 January, Eric was once again detailed for duties as Master Bomber, this time a return to Politz. Eric was happy to discover over the target that the weather conditions were much better than forecast and the initial plan to mark blind was abandoned in favour of marking visually. Low-level marking executed by 627 was deemed highly accurate, and despite issues reported with the wind vectors being used to set up the Main Force bombsights, the subsequent bombing by a force of more than 200 Lancasters, reduced the oil plant 'to a shambles'.[69]

A few days later, on Tuesday 16 January, Eric was in action as Master Bomber once more and to another synthetic oil plant far to the East. Brux (also known as Most to Czech-speaking people), in Western Czechoslovakia, had been producing synthetic oil since the beginning of 1943, employing labour from a subcamp of the Sachsenhausen Concentration Camp. It had been a favourite target of the USAAF since the early summer of 1944 and now Eric was being given the chance to finish it off. He did not squander the opportunity. Controlling a force of 231 Lancasters from Nos 1 and 5 Groups, Eric found the target covered in fog but it proved not to be an issue. The Green proximity markers were dropped with considerable accuracy and some of the No. 627 Squadron Mosquitoes were able to identify and mark the target visually. Aware that the glow of the Red TIs would not be seen by all, and may soon disappear, he could be heard repeatedly calling 'Sky Sky Sky' which was answered with a cascade of Wanganui flares. Now he could give Main Force the option and instructed them to aim either at the sky markers or the red glow of the TIs if visible. The result was near total destruction. A huge explosion lit up the night sky and a characteristic mushroom cloud of oily black smoke began billowing from the plant. Albert Speer, the Nazi Armaments Minister would subsequently mention this raid as causing a particularly severe setback to Germany's oil production.

(Many years later, in 2002, Eric's daughter Jeannie would receive a letter, completely out of the blue, from Radovan Helt a Czech historian, referring to this raid and thanking her for the very accurate bombing of the German Oil Industry at Brux carried out by her father in 1945.)

Before leaving for Brux, Eric had hung around in the Mess on the off chance that he might hear from Betty but fancied that all incoming/outgoing calls would be subject to secrecy regulations. He hoped too they might speak the next evening but doubted he could get away from a 'Dining in' night at the Mess. They had recently bid farewell to Sir Ralph Cochrane and welcomed a new AOC, Hugh Constantine. Cochrane was something of a cold fish who many, including Eric, found difficult to like but whose Commander-in-Chief, Harris, recognised as one of his ablest leaders. Constantine was far more approachable, perhaps because unlike Cochrane he had flown operationally. He had commanded No. 214 Squadron earlier in the war and as Station Commander at RAF Elsham Wolds had taken part in the first of the thousand bomber raids. Eric wrote about both men, and his recent exertions, in his letter to Betty on the afternoon of 17 January. He was also delighted to bump into his old 'boss' from 150 days, Bill Hesketh:

> Again, I haven't been able to write for two days and I fear you were disappointed last night. I expect you tried to get through. I don't know if they do allow incoming calls on a 'working night', but I was working, anyway. I went to Czecho-Slovakia – BRUX – so I was a long way away! Actually, I was in the Mess until 7.15, just in the hope, but then I had to get cracking. I hope we are lucky tonight. The only trick is that it is a Dining In night and very official. I might have to ask an Air Vice Marshal to excuse me, if your call comes. So think yourself honoured.
>
> I've been 'in' with the Brass Hats quite a bit lately. A conference at Group on Monday was to say goodbye to our present AOC (that old waxen-faced johnny). It lasted from 3-00 till 7-00pm, including drinks on him and introduction to the new AOC who is far more 'human'. 'Wotcha-chum' sort-of-thing. I had quite a chat with him, stroking him

the right way. Lots of people were there. Bill Hesketh was and he said rather a nice thing. As I was going, he sent his love to you and said as I was going through the door 'I'm very proud of you, Benjie!' I saw quite a lot in that remark. He's a grand fellow.

The senior M.B. (Master Bomber) took me round to some 'public' friends of his in Lincoln after the conference and we beered a little until 10pm.

I got back from last night's op at 1.30, bed at 3.30, was up at 8.30 and am flying in an hour's time, as the weather's nice. So I'm a bit busy. As I shall be very occupied tonight, I thought I must write now. I've got to sit next to an AVM (air vice marshal) tonight. There are going to be 2 AVMs, 3 A/Cdrs (air commodores) and 8 G/Cs (group captains)! Bags of Braid and B's.h.i.t!

His thoughts also turned to the imminent arrival of his second child:

There's so much about our dear little thing in your letters, I don't know what to say. She gets sweeter & sweeter. Talk about dreams! You and yours! I had a terribly real one. Never had such a real one in my life. I woke up with it and couldn't get it out of my mind – I felt it was true! About three nights ago I dreamed I got a phone call to say you had had a boy! It was real. Well, we're having some bad luck with the phone, now, aren't we, but perhaps I'll get it, tonight. I do hope so, because it might be the last before our little one arrives.

Bye bye for now, my love, and don't get 'worked up'. Try to have just that little bit of courage I have to cling to on my 'ops'.

Like many pilots during the war and afterwards, Eric felt tremendous affection for the Mosquito. It was sturdy, reliable and served him well. Such was his devotion to this aircraft that when it was featured on the cover of the monthly Aeroplane magazine he wrote to the aircraft manufacturer, De Havilland, requesting a copy of the picture – a highly stylised colour image of two mosquitoes racing across the night sky.[70]

While waiting to do some local flying in the early evening of 21 January, he penned a short note to Betty making mention of his request and a visit by the founder of the RAF, Lord Trenchard, to No. 54 Base:

I'm going on a spot of local flying in ½hr. & then to the local on a Sunday evening 'social' gathering, so here's a short line as there's not much news.

The great Lord Trenchard, Marshal of the RAF, visited us yesterday. I didn't see him, though. There was a lot of misunderstanding of his plans and in the end I discovered I was supposed to dine with him and a crowd, but it was too late – they had dined. It didn't matter.

I wrote to De Havilland Aircraft for a picture of a Mosquito I saw on the cover of the 'Aeroplane' about a fortnight ago and have just received a magnificent picture about two feet square, free of charge. It's a beautiful thing in colour against a cloud background and will make a lovely picture for us when I get a good home for it. Wasn't it good of them? They have put me on a 'list' for further pictures!

He also explained why he had not been operating much recently, and was at pains to re-assure Betty lest their future communications be interrupted:

Well, Angel, there's plenty of snow around and we're not 'working' lately, but I hope it doesn't happen again this Tuesday as last. If it does, Angel, and you don't get through Wednesday, just try Thursday as well, eh, 'cause this is a special week. If you're at all 'groggy', though, please don't. In case we don't get through, then, just remember I shall be with you every single moment, Angel, these coming days.

It is not surprising that there was some 'misunderstanding' regarding Lord Trenchard's plans. He arrived at RAF Metheringham after lunch and began chatting to various aircrew before dining at RAF Coningsby with a 'crowd', to which Eric refers, comprising the Base commander, station commanders, squadron commanders, flight commanders and senior staff officers of the Base. He then gave 'a stimulating and interesting address' to aircrew officers and NCOs assembled in the ante-room.[71]

Betty was now within days of giving birth and she was still making her weekly visit to the telephone box in the cold to hear her husband's voice. Uppermost in their minds was the name they were going to give to their new baby. Betty was considering calling the new baby Margaret, but Eric was firmly fixed on the name Sally Ann. They seemed pretty sure it would be another girl. Shortly after writing to Betty in the early evening of 23rd, they managed to speak on the phone:

Well, my darling, that was lovely. There was little to say, but we said it and it made all the difference. You must have been cold, though. I hope you hurried home and got warm. (Of course you did.) I've been just nattering away the evening and am now listening to the wireless in the warmth of my room.

In the same letter, Eric also referenced the attack on Brux, and was rather pleased with the result:

> Here's some 'gratifying' news on last Tuesday. That long journey was certainly not in vain for, as a result of my 'master' controlling, photographic pictures taken after the raid have proved the op. to have been a big success! The news came through yesterday and I was quite bucked. You get a feeling of anxious suspense after an op., wondering what the actual results really were, even if you see fires at the time. I'm now waiting to see the pictures, if we get them. What a 'morbid' husband you've got! I shall be thrilled to bits to see the place devastated and I can say – 'I did that!' Isn't it terrible?

The attacks on Politz and Brux were a continuation of the Directive given to Bomber Command to prioritise oil targets but Harris still had his eye on bombing German cities when the opportunity arose, especially to support the Russian advance. On 27 January 1945, Soviet troops liberated Auschwitz, the death camp synonymous with the Holocaust and the attempted annihilation of the Jews. As a paid-up member of the Communist Party Betty's father, 'Pop', was a big supporter of the Russians and when the horrors of this place became known to the world, he took a special pride in their achievement. As Eric noted:

> Aren't the Russians doing well? Pop's 'master plan' is gradually coming into effect, I suppose. Give him my congratulations and point out that my part in recent operations has had a very material, almost direct, effect on Russian advances.

Three days later, on Tuesday 30 January, while Eric was still at RAF Coningsby, Betty was admitted to the West Middlesex Hospital and gave birth to their second child, Sally, the following day. Mam and Pop accompanied her. Winnie stayed at home to look after Jeannie, who was now almost 18 months and growing up fast. Eric received the phone call with the joyous news and immediately celebrated in the Mess. While there were no complications, Betty remained in hospital for ten days, which was common practice at the time. Eric was not due to see her and his new baby until she came out of hospital, but he was able to speak to her on the phone and the letters continued to flow. At the end of his next letter (4 February) there was now not one extra kiss but two, one for Jeannie and one for Sally.

> How are you doing, now? Won't be long, now, before I'll be fetching you. Good, eh?
> A little girl of ten, known by a WAAF officer, here, heard her mother talking about a man who was being buried. She at once

exclaimed: 'He's on the adding-up, Mummy.' What did she mean? He's on the plus sign (+). He's on the cross (x). He's dead! Oi!

A party, last night. Swinderby. Jealous? Actually, it was pretty dull. My stomach was a tiny bit out of order and I only drank a couple of pints and a couple of gins. Still, it made a change. The food was not a bit up to usual standard. I retired at 2-00am. And slept very well.

Arrangements were made for Eric to fetch Betty from the hospital, a happy occasion that coincided with confirmation of Eric's promotion to wing commander, backdated to 1 January. Dennis Stubbs was also promoted, both men being called in to see the Base Commander. The wheels of authority had turned only very slowly given that their role as Master Bombers was clearly stated as a wing commander's post. It was clear, also, that there was some disagreement among the senior commanders as to the qualifying criteria for a Controller to be given wing commander status. Eric hinted at the behind-the-scenes squabbles in his letter of 6 February:

> Well, news. There has been considerable doubt for some time on if and when our W/Co was coming through. By 'our', I mean another S/L Master Bomber. The last AOC suddenly changed his mind about the number of qualifying trips or something and there was considerable argument about it. Anyway, the Base Commander had us in today and gave us the good news that at last the AOC was agreeable and we were put up for it today. It should come through in a week or two and will then be back-dated to 1st Jan. They have done us out of a little money, as we've held the post since 26th October. However, it'll be rather nice. Another 5/4 a day.

Eric's promotion meant a welcome uplift in pay, and talk also shifted to the issue of war gratuities, a one-off lump sum payment made to those who served in the armed forces, and how much he could expect after the war:

> What d'you think of the war gratuities? Shocking, aren't they? If I qualify by staying in the service, I shall get about £125. I'm not sure they'll give anything to us if we stay in the service, though.

Eric had every reason to be thinking of the future. He now had Betty and Sally safely home at 23 Mays Road and mother and baby were doing well. He was given ten days' leave to bond with his new daughter now that his family of three had become a family of four. Proud of his recent promotion, he insisted that he sew the third thick ring (to denote his wing commander's rank) on to his uniform himself, using Betty's mother's old sewing machine. He said it would be unlucky if anyone else were to do it.

The day before his return to Base he and Betty posed with their two children for a photograph in the garden of their home. It would be the only photograph of the four of them together. Although Betty later said that she wished Eric hadn't been in his shirt sleeves she nevertheless pasted it proudly in the family album after the war, drawing a series of flamboyant wavy rings around it.

On Sunday 18 February, Eric returned to RAF Coningsby. While he had been away, Maurice Smith, one of his fellow Controllers, had been busy. On the night of 13/14 February he'd controlled the raid on Dresden, a vital communications and supply centre to German forces on the Eastern Front. It was one of several cities identified (including Berlin, Leipzig and Chemnitz) to be hit in direct support of Soviet troops on the ground as part of 'Operation Thunderclap'. The raid was devastating; tens of thousands died in two raids on the city, the first being a wholly No. 5 Group affair. The destruction was so total that the true purpose and morality of the raids have been questioned ever since.

After lunch on the nineteenth, Eric wrote what would be his last letter to his wife, a letter she would receive after his death:

Hullo My Love,

I thought I must drop you a line, now, as I felt like it. Before I tell you about the journey, etc., I want to say it was a simply beautiful leave – so complete with you and our children – he! It's so difficult to leave you, though. That last two minutes is awful, isn't it? Still, we mustn't dwell on it. I'm back on the job, again and we must get used to writing letters and looking forward to next time.

I made very good time and got to Peterborough at 7-00 where I had a nice supper of plaice and veg. I made the camp at 9.15, which was very good going, wasn't it? I had to pay the Mess a visit and buy a round, of course, to celebrate. I turned in at 11-00 and had a good night. The baby didn't cry – or did she?

I found a letter from Desmond in the wrack – just to say how do. In fact, here it is, which please return. Yes, I did forget my pipe and baccy! I thought I had it in my pocket. I expect you're sending it. Tell Pop that Dresden was hit really hard just as the newspapers and Jerry say. He was wanting to know. The Russians will be able to go forward again, now!

Every bit of my love, Angel, to you and quite a bit for those kids of ours!

On the morning of 19 February, at the headquarters of Bomber Command at High Wycombe, Arthur Harris held his usual 'morning prayers', meeting with his senior staff officers to discuss the results of the previous night's efforts before considering a new target for his forces to attack. While he thought very little of the official directive to concentrate on oil and transportation, he nonetheless was obliged to follow orders, and after taking counsel from various specialists, including the chief Met man, decided upon Böhlen as his preferred 'target for tonight'. It was home to the Braunkohle-Benzin synthetic oil refinery, some seven miles south of Leipzig, and not far from the plant at Brux where Eric had enjoyed earlier success. It had also been attacked a few days earlier, though escaped serious damage. Harris also selected smaller targets, among them Erfurt, for a series of 'siren raids' (i.e raids to keep the sirens wailing over Germany) by Mosquitoes of No. 8 Group's Light Night Striking Force.

The meeting lasted little more than twenty minutes before Harris departed, leaving his Deputy, Robert Saundby, to handle the detail. A call was put through to No. 5 Group at Morton Hall via scrambler phone with news of the target, and the subsequent timing, marking and routing for the attack was left to the discretion of the No. 5 Group AOC, Hugh Constantine. A Flight Planning Conference was held, linking the Group to its Base stations, by which time the Master Bomber, Eric, had been appointed and the timing for the early evening briefings of captains and crews were set. By 10.30am, the various squadrons taking part had received their operational orders including the numbers of Lancasters they were expected to provide, and the groundcrews set to work preparing their aircraft. Take-off times for the heavy Pathfinders of Nos 83 and 97 Squadrons and Main Force crews was to be around midnight, and for the Mosquitoes of No. 627 Squadron, nearer two in the morning. H-Hour (the time for the bombing to begin) was set for 04.15.

Around 01.30, Eric and Jack, in full flying kit, and having collected their escape kits and signed for their parachutes, made their way to their Mosquito, a MkXXV with the Serial No KB401. It carried the No. 627 Squadron code, 'AZ', and the individual aircraft identifier 'E'. It was Eric's 'regular' aircraft, albeit on loan from his friends at RAF Woodhall Spa. The MkXXV was a significant upgrade on the Canadian built MkXX with improved single-stage Packard Merlin 225 piston engines. Having had one final look at the outsides of the aircraft, ensuring all the locks and covers have been removed and having tested the flying surfaces to make sure they were clear of obstructions, the two men climbed in. Eric carefully placed the small mascot of a child's teddy bear in its usual place. They went through their pre-flight checks with considered thoroughness. Take off time arrived and the first of the engines fired into life, quickly followed by the second. Eric pushed the throttles forward and watched the temperatures creeping up. Then he opened both engines up full bore prior to throttling back to taxi. All was well with the world. Taxiing to the start of their take off run they awaited the blink of light from the Aldis lamp held by the man in Flying Control. Then they were away, the time recorded at 01.55.

The flight out was uneventful, perhaps even a little routine. Jack had no problems navigating them to their target, and they arrived early as did the other Mosquitoes of Marker force. Perhaps predictably the target was covered in a thick blanket of 10/10ths cloud but Eric wasn't particularly concerned. They were ready for such an eventuality and some of the marker Mosquitoes carried Wanganui flares to be used as a last resort if needed.[72]

The first of the Green Target Indicators from the blind marker force went down, albeit a little late, and Eric appeared satisfied, issuing the first of his instructions for the markers to be backed up. Illumination of the target was initially poor, the illuminators having dropped their flares too early and some way to the east of the target, but one of the No. 627 Squadron Mosquitoes got a good sight of some of the factory towers and placed a Red TI on what he took to be the middle of the target.

Eric orbited the scene beneath the cloud and called in Main Force to bomb, but not all Main Force crews could see the marker he was referring to. Some expected Eric to revert to a Wanganui, the fall-back marking technique when the target was covered in cloud, but no such instruction was given. Others expected an order to come down beneath the cloud, and some took it upon themselves to do just that, not waiting to be told to descend lower than the briefed height.

The Germans began filling the sky with heavy and predicted flak. Several of the Lancasters were hit as the others awaited further commentary. Moments after issuing his last instruction, Eric's Mosquito too was hit, and some heard him on VHF call out: 'Oh Damn, I've been hit. I'm going down. Number two take over, number two take over....'

Not everyone heard his message, and for a few short seconds the Marker Leader, Rupert Oakley[73] could be heard trying to make contact with Eric before issuing his own order first to bomb the Greens and then quickly correcting himself to aim at the Reds. It was not quite clear who was now in charge, a fact confirmed by Fraser Muir, a member of the RCAF in another aircraft on the same operation: 'A voice came on stating that he was number two, followed by a second voice claiming that he was number two, then all hell broke loose with a lot of yelling and clear chaos.'

The attack which had started out well enough now quickly descended into a free-for-all, their trouble compounded by a third voice now on the airwaves. It was a German pretending to be in charge but largely ignored for failing to use the word 'Smokey', the agreed call-sign for Main Force. Some crews could just discern the glow of the reds through the cloud and the blinking explosions of bombs below, and turned for home, happy with their efforts. Others considered the raid a dismal failure, and that good initial marking had been wasted for failing to bring the Main Force where they could see the target visually.[74]

Eric's Mosquito crashed near Koltzschen, a quiet hamlet some six kilometres south of Colditz and its famous castle. Neither man had time to escape and the local fire services took some time to extinguish the flames. Despite Wing Commander Oakley's swift intervention, the attack was not a success. Bombing was scattered and the damage merely superficial. All 254 heavy bombers returned home safely, as did the No. 627 Squadron Mosquitoes. KB401 was the only aircraft that failed to return.

A few hours later and several hundred miles away, Betty was listening earnestly to the radio while breastfeeding her three-week old daughter. She was relieved to hear on the one o'clock news that only two aircraft had failed to return from the previous night's raid. In fact, there was only one aircraft lost, her husband's. An hour later, there was a knock at the front door. It was what every wife, mother or father feared: a telegram to say their loved one was missing. She had received such a telegram before, five years earlier when Eric had been shot down in France, but this time there was to be no happy ending.

After the official telegram, and as was customary, Betty received a follow-up letter from Eric's commanding officer, the No. 54 Base Commander Harry Satterly. Satterly was hopeful that Eric may still have been alive, given his flying skills:

Dear Mrs Benjamin,

I would like to offer my sympathy and that of all the personnel of my Command in the sorrow which must be yours on receiving the news that your husband, Wing Commander Benjamin, failed to return from an operational flight.

He was the pilot of an aircraft detailed to carry out an attack on the night of 19th/20th February, 1945. It may well be that he had an opportunity to bail out or that the aircraft crash landed in enemy territory and I sincerely hope that such is the case. As you know he had considerable experience and would make the most of every chance far more readily than most other people, especially as he was so cool and calm in the air. You will, of course, be notified immediately when any further news is forthcoming.

I have known your husband for quite a long time now and I expect you know he had been carefully selected for important duties. He was most popular with everyone who knew him and we shall all miss him both for his splendid and gallant work and in the mess.

He came and told me proudly a little while ago about his new daughter – Sally – because he knew I have a daughter with the same name.

I hope you will soon hear more cheerful news of him and if he should be a prisoner of war, it cannot be more than a few weeks or months before this European war ends and he is back with you and the family once again.

The reason for the request in my telegram notifying you that your husband was missing was to prevent his chance of escape being prejudiced by undue publication in case he is still at large. I do not wish to convey the idea that any more information about him is available, but this request is a precaution adopted in the case of all personnel reported missing.

If there is anything at all I can do....

Betty wrote back to Air Commodore Satterly, beseeching him for more details about that fateful night. She received an immediate reply:

Dear Mrs Benjamin,

Thank you very much for your letter and I am only too sorry that I cannot give you any more information which would help you at present. Not through unwillingness of course but merely because there is no more information to give.

He did not say he was baling out or, if he did, he was not heard but if someone else was talking at the same time from another aircraft then he would not be heard. We frequently get two messages jamming each other but whether this happened on this particular occasion I do not know. He would certainly have plenty of height to bail out always provided of course that he did not waste a lot of time about it and I think he was much too quick witted for that. If he did have to bail out very quickly he would not of course spend valuable seconds trying to get a message through.

The risk as I see it is that he may have sustained a direct hit but the chance of this happening is small. A more serious risk is that he might have been knocked out first by a stray piece of flak.

I am sure you will appreciate that this is all guesswork on my part and must remain so until we get more news but I have tried to give you both sides of the picture as they appear to me.

I do not want to raise false hopes but neither should you be too despondent. There is always hope that he is a prisoner of war or even trying to find his way back to this country unless and until we get news to the contrary – and I do most sincerely hope it will be brighter news when it comes. It often takes a long time before we hear although you would wish to know that the longer it takes the less likely is the chance of escape. It normally takes between two and eight weeks before we get any news at all.

In the subsequent weeks Betty continued desperately to seek out information wherever she could. She received many letters from friends, who tried to reassure her. One recounted the story of another airman who had been missing for eight weeks before he was eventually confirmed safe as a prisoner of war. Another reminded Betty of how Eric had gone missing before and no harm had come to him. Bill Hesketh was cautiously optimistic that Eric was still alive, but also keen that Betty should be prepared for the worst. He wrote:

> Air Commodore Satterly has phoned me to say that he had heard from you, and that you were enquiring for confirmation of some unconfirmed information which I mentioned to Mrs Long.
> The facts are as follows. Knowing that Benny was controlling that night and that he had not returned – when I went to see my own crews I made enquiries of them as to what they had heard over the radio. From two separate sources I heard that someone, thought to be Benny, had been heard to say that he had had an engine knocked out of action and that he would have to hand over to his Deputy.

In the months that followed, Betty spent many more hours writing letters to the authorities, attempting to obtain further information about her husband's fate. She recalled those days in her life story written in 1991:

> He went back on the 18th February and was posted missing on the 19th. Black, black days and nights, hoping against hope that he was in enemy hands. All the family a wonderful support and grieving with me. What a comfort my babies were – life had to go on – a daily round of feeding and nappies.

Exactly eleven weeks after Eric was killed, the war in Europe came to an end. While others celebrated and partied, Betty sat miserably at home with her two little daughters and her grief. Neither Eric's lucky mascot, nor his lucky Service Number 77777, had spared him. As Betty tried desperately to cling on to the last vestiges of hope, these were finally dashed in July 1945 when she received the following letter from the Director of Personal Services at the Air Ministry Casualty Branch:

I am directed to refer to your letter dated the 21st June, 1945, regarding your husband, Acting Wing Commander Eric Arthur Benjamin DFC, (77777) Royal Air Force, and to inform you that a detailed report has now been received from the Squadron.

This report states that your husband's aircraft took off from base at 1.55am. on the 20th February, 1945, to carry out an attack against Böhlen, and was last heard on the radio when over the target area at approximately 4.05am. An aircraft was seen to hit the ground four miles north-east of the target, but it is not known whether this was the aircraft in which your husband was flying.

As all Air Force personnel who were evading or captured are in Allied hands and the majority have now returned to the United Kingdom it is felt that had your husband been safe, official notification would have been received by now and you yourself would have heard direct from him.

It should be explained, that as soon as local conditions permit, the Royal Air Force Missing Research and Enquiry Service (MRES) is being established in order to pursue enquiries for all Air Force personnel reported missing and about whom no news has been received. However, in view of the magnitude of the task, some time must necessarily elapse before complete information becomes available.

Meanwhile, I am to extend to you the sincere sympathy of the Department in your anxiety, and to assure you that you will be informed with the least possible delay, should any further news come to hand.

In the intervening period, Eric's body had been recovered from the crash and buried in the cemetery at nearby Colditz. Sadly, the body of his navigator, Jack Heath, was never found. It is likely that the intensity of the flames consumed his mortal remains, such that nothing was left that could be identified.

In Betty's memoir, written in her later years, she states that a year after Eric's death she had already accepted that her husband had been killed. Writing to Eric's uncle and aunt in Canada on 11 January 1946, however, she seemed far from accepting of his fate:

Dear Uncle Leslie and Aunt Maud,

I'm afraid this letter will not be a happy one so please forgive me if I sound stilted and disjointed. I have never written to you before of course, as that was always Eric's pleasure. If only I didn't have to say this – even now I can hardly bear to write it – it's like a hideous nightmare. Eric has been presumed killed on a raid over Böhlen (nr Leipzig) on Feb 20th last year. He was reported missing at first and I was so sure he would turn up – I just lived on hope for eight months and then they presumed him killed. But I don't know any details at all. The worry and grief have nearly driven me off my head and poor Eric's mother too, needless to say. She bore up very well at first, as, like me, she was full of hope, but I'm afraid it seems against all reason to hope any longer. I just cannot bring myself to accept it though and will never be able to think of him as really gone.

The babies are all I live for now, - nothing seems worthwhile except them. I don't know if you knew there was going to be another one? I had another girl, Sally Ann on Jan 31st '45. Eric saw her just once and went missing the night after his return from leave.

Jeannie gets more like him every day – Sally is more like me. Eric's mother is living at Addlestone with her mother at present. (Still alive and kicking at 89!) Ernest is still in India and Leslie in Germany (he will be demobbed in March).

I hope you are all well. Eric's mother sends her kindest regards and hopes you will forgive her not writing.

In response she received a letter from Eric's other uncle and aunt in Winnipeg, Canada, Arthur and Levina, the ones to whom he had written in 1937 and declared that 'there is no greater sport than flying'.

It was with deepest regret that we have heard of your sad loss and words now fail to express our condolences at the grief we know you must feel.

I received a letter from Eric that he wrote just before that last mission. In the letter he mentioned his joy at the birth of the little girl.

Leslie and Maud gave us your letter to read and it certainly came as a shock. Levina and our children unite with me in this expression of sympathy. Please convey this message to Eric's mother and brothers and sister.

We are truly sorry to re-open this wound but would feel delinquent if we let it pass without comment.

P.S. I am passing the news to Eric's Aunt Rose at Stoughton in Surrey.

In March 1946 Betty received a formal request to attend Buckingham Palace to receive from the hands of the King the medals conferred on her husband, the DFC and Bar. It stated clearly that children under seven years of age may not attend and so, accompanied by her mother-in-law on 9 April 1946 she duly attended the Palace on Eric's behalf. Notwithstanding her pride in Eric's bravery, what should have been a day of joy with her husband was instead one of sadness and despair.

After the war, on 26 September 1947, Eric's body was recovered by a unit of the MRES, and his identity confirmed. It was a grim but necessary task carried out by small groups of ordinary RAF airmen who had little or no training for the role but were quick to learn. His remains were exhumed from the Colditz cemetery and reverently reinterred in the British Military Cemetery at Charlottenburg in Berlin, in Plot 1, Row Z, Grave 13. The headstone was inscribed with the words:

UNTIL WE MEET AGAIN.
BETTY, JEANNE AND SALLY

(Betty's mother commissioned the inscription and always spelled Jeannie's name without the 'i').

Jack Heath is commemorated along with thousands of others who have no known grave at the Runnymede Memorial. His name is carved on Panel No. 267. His life is also remembered on a local war memorial in Samlesbury, Lancashire.

After her husband's death Betty dedicated her life to her daughters. As she wrote:

> From then on my life was totally centred on two little girls – my pride and joy – and the years flew. First Communions, Confirmations, birthday parties, open days and sports days – always lovingly attended by 'the family' – overwhelmingly so as recently admitted by Jeannie and Sally. 'Other girls' parents came, but we had hordes of relatives!'

When she was in her early thirties Betty went to a dance and met Fred Ridge. Fred was keen for them to marry but Betty's fierce love for her two daughters was such that nothing and no-one could disturb the family unit and Fred had to wait until Jeannie and Sally had themselves married and left home before Betty finally agreed to wed. There was another, more practical reason for the delay. If she were to marry again, she would lose her RAF widow's pension. She married Fred in 1968 when she was fifty. They moved to a bungalow in Steyning, Sussex and made a good life for themselves.

Of Eric's daughters, Jeannie married in 1966 and Sally the following year. In her later years, Betty devoted her time to her four grandchildren:

> My happy granny days started in September 1966 with Dylan, Charlotte in February 1968, Toby in January 1972 and a wonderful little late

arrival, Rebecca in December 1979, 'year of the child'. Have had enormous pleasure from them all, and my two loving daughters, and am having a very happy old age! All this, and Heaven too?!!

In 1987 she and Fred, with the aid of the Royal British Legion and Government sponsors, were able to visit Eric's grave at Charlottenburg. It was a pilgrimage Betty had waited forty-two years to make, and it was again another occasion of great sadness and pride as she placed a poppy wreath against Eric's gravestone. The visit comprised a party of twenty-two war widows and was reported in their local newspaper. As Betty remarked at the time, 'The years just fell away. The ceremony in the cemetery was very moving.'

Very sadly, in 1991 at the age of 73 and not long after writing the last few pages of her life story, Betty was killed in a car crash. It was only seven months after Fred had died of cancer and she was on her way to keep an appointment with her solicitor to sign a new will. Her car was in a head-on collision with a lorry coming in the opposite direction. She left a letter for her two daughters to read after her death, in which she said she hoped they wouldn't have to read for many years to come. At the end of that letter, she added an appendix with a few copied quotations from Eric's letters:

Forty years since the telegram came and ended my happy carefree youth. My babies of three weeks and eighteen months now middle aged and my darling is still twenty-five – age did not weary him nor the years condemn. (He did not grow fat either or lose his teeth.) The years that I wished away with such a fierce young grief have passed. I have been re-reading for the millionth time his happy and concerned young letters. The letters never fail to bring him and those times vividly to mind:

'It was lovely to hear you on the phone, sorry to hear about the bad raids'
'You must take care not to slip on the icy roads now your time is getting near'
'Shall be Officer Commanding night flying tonight so may not be able to receive your call'
'Did a trip last night and didn't get to bed till 5 o'clock – hope to get a few days leave, but don't get too excited in case.'
'Went to the cinema – 1/- seats, tell Mum'
'Batman allowance of 2/- per day'

So long ago but it still feels like yesterday.

Afterword

By Jeannie Benjamin

On Thursday 28 June 2012, the day after what would have been my father's ninety-third birthday, the Dedication of the Bomber Command Memorial in London's The Green Park took place. A sculpture of a bomber air crew was unveiled by Her Majesty the Queen and the ceremony was attended by thousands of veterans and relatives of the 55,573 airmen who gave their lives serving in Bomber Command during the Second World War. As next of kin to one of those airmen I was invited to attend. I proudly wore my father's medal, the DFC & Bar and that day was one of the most poignant days of my life. I shed many tears as a Lancaster bomber dropped thousands of poppies over Green Park in a salute to those young men. For me it was the funeral my father had never had.

  It was an unexpectedly hot day and bottles of water were being handed out to the crowd by members of the RAF Benevolent Fund. I felt a special affection for that organisation as it had paid for my sister's and my education. As I sat there in the crowd I was very aware of the very many veterans around me, men in their late eighties and nineties, proudly wearing their heavy air-force blue uniforms and wilting in the heat, some of them struggling to stand. I tried to imagine my father as an old man but it was impossible; he would always be a handsome twenty-five-year old. I was unaware that among that vast crowd was another old man whose birthday had also been on the previous day and who had a special connection to my father. I wasn't to find this out until a month later.

  I was travelling home to Reading from Kent along the M25 when I received a text message from my sister, Sally. She told me that she had received a message on Facebook from a man we had never heard of, a Canadian called Fraser Muir, telling her that he had heard our father's last words, spoken as his aircraft was shot down over Germany in February 1945. She had read those words and was in tears. This came as a complete shock both to her and to me. I was thunderstruck. It was sixty-seven years since our father had been killed and now we were being informed that not only had our father spoken in his last few minutes but that those words had been heard by someone who was still alive and who had been trying to contact us for many years. It was almost too surreal to believe.

As soon as I arrived home I switched on my computer, heart racing, and logged into my Facebook account. There they were, those few last words uttered by my father:

> 'Oh Damn, I've been hit. I'm going down. Number two take over, number two take over…..'

Just a few prosaic words, saying so little but so very much.

I was now crying with a grief which was coming up from somewhere very deep inside my being. My father was speaking to me beyond the grave all these years later. I was at that moment no longer a woman approaching her sixty-ninth birthday but an eighteen-month-old toddler crying for her daddy. I let the tears flow.

Afterwards came the questions. Who was this man who was telling us this amazing news? How had he come to hear those words? Why hadn't he told us before? Why did he want to tell us now? How did he find us? The answers emerged gradually through Facebook messages and emails during the next few weeks.

Fraser Muir was a mid-upper gunner in the Royal Canadian Air Force. In the Second World War he was posted to No. 5 Group Bomber Command, the same group as my father's. On the night of 19 February 1945 they had both been on the same bombing mission, a raid on the synthetic oil plan at Böhlen, near Leipzig. Fraser had not known my father personally but when he heard those words uttered over the VHF radio that night he said he was amazed by the sound of my father's voice; he said there was no panic, no shouting and he 'seemed to be more concerned with his responsibility of passing on his command to Number Two than the fact he was on the way down'.

Fraser went on to say, 'It was the calm, collected, controlled nature of his voice that has made it one of the most vivid memories of my tour of thirty-five bombing operations'.

Fraser wondered for many years whether my father had survived that night and a couple of years before the Bomber Command Memorial Unveiling he found a copy of *The Bomber Command War Diaries* at a book sale. There he discovered that the Master Bomber leading that raid that night was Wing Commander E.A. Benjamin, DFC & Bar, and that he was buried in the Berlin War Cemetery. Fraser said:

AFTERWORD

To say I was saddened to learn that he had died is an understatement. At every Mass I have attended over the years, (and I have attended many!) I have included him in my prayers said with those for my fallen comrades. Each time I hoped that he may well have gone down but survived the hit.

My sister and I gradually learned how he had tracked us down. He had attended the unveiling ceremony in 2012 as part of a delegation of Canadian veterans and after returning to Canada had seen a comment I had made on the Bomber Command Memorial Facebook page. He had seen my father's name along with mine and he sent me a private Facebook message. However, I was quite a novice Facebook user in those days and did not see the message so when he received no reply he checked my Facebook friends and eventually managed to contact Sally.

Fraser said he was ecstatic in finding 'his Master Bomber's' family. He went on to say:

Another interesting connection that I have with W/C Benjamin is that we both share the same birthday…..June 27th. At the time of the bombing over Böhlen he was twenty-five and I was twenty. May he rest in peace eternally.

It took many months for the enormity of this discovery to sink in. I was trying to process the information that throughout my whole life there had been someone in another continent, exactly five years younger than my father, who had heard his final words and been so affected by them that he had been constantly praying for him and keeping him in his thoughts. And when he finally learned that my father had indeed died on that day and had left a wife and two children it was his earnest hope that one day he would be able to let us know what those words were. Through the providence of Facebook this had now happened.

During the next few years after the unveiling of the Bomber Command Memorial Fraser and I continued a regular correspondence through email and Facebook, always expressing the wish that one day we might actually meet each other. Towards the end of 2014 Fraser told me that the following May there was to be a celebration in a town called Apeldoorn to mark the 70th anniversary of the Liberation of the Netherlands and there was a possibility that he and his wife Joan would be attending. They would be part of a delegation organised by the Canadian organisation 'Veteran Affairs'. I asked him to keep me informed as I would love to take the opportunity of meeting him there. As the spring of 2015 approached it became more apparent that this would now become a reality.

At the end of March Fraser informed me that they would be in Holland from 2nd until 10th May, saying that, 'As soon as I'm advised the complete information I'll advise you....I look forward to our meeting....it's almost an unbelievable 'Happening'....'

He then sent me their schedule and the name of two hotels in Apeldoorn (it had not been decided which one they would be staying in) and on 12th April I booked my flight and a hotel which was near to both as the two he mentioned were fully booked with their delegation. This was Fraser's response: 'Great News....Excited too!....I think it's a fantastic 'Happening'....I too am looking forward to meeting you Jeannie Dear...'

In the next exchange Fraser suggested I submit a write-up of our story to a project he himself had contributed to in which he recounts at length his memory of the night he heard my father's words and which he had entitled One in a Million. I agreed and responded with a suggestion of my own, that during our forthcoming meeting I would like to ask someone to make a short video of him talking to me about that night in February 1945 and how he subsequently found me and my sister on Facebook. This was his enthusiastic reply:

> My Darling Girl....I would welcome it with open arms....I've been waiting for the moment we'll meet for 70 years, more or less....of course it should be recorded. Can't wait....can't be soon enough....to capture, not only me on camera....but us!!!

2015. Tuesday 5th May

I set off from Reading with huge excitement and some degree of anxiety. I enjoy travelling on my own, nevertheless the prospect of making my way independently across Holland by train did feel a little daunting. Some years previously, in December 2004, my sister and I had travelled together to visit our father's grave in Berlin. It was the first time we had seen his grave and it was a very moving occasion. I had hoped she and I would again travel together but unfortunately this time she was unable to join me. However, she was with me in spirit all the way.

I was travelling from Terminal 5 at Heathrow, which I always find exciting. I had plenty of time to spare before my flight and I sat by a window overlooking the planes taking off and landing while I did the Guardian crossword. A young woman sitting next to me leaned across and asked if I would help her daughter with her word puzzle. We began talking and she told me she was going to Berlin. I said that was where my father was buried and began telling her the story about my father and Fraser Muir. When I had finished she looked at me and said it had made her quite teary.

AFTERWORD

I have found that it often has this effect on people. My flight was called and we said goodbye.

It was a very short flight to Amsterdam. I barely had time to drink my complimentary Gin and Tonic. As the plane was landing I was able to see the Rijksmuseum from my window seat. I found this very thrilling as I had visited that splendid building the previous September. I arrived at Schiphol Airport at 6.35pm local time and after collecting my baggage I emerged out of the arrivals hall into an enormous shopping mall. I had no idea where to find the train for the next part of my journey to Apeldoorn. After asking various people for help (I was so thankful that the Dutch all speak English) I eventually located the platform and settled down for an hour long train journey, the same length of time as the flight had taken.

As the train sped through the flat plains of Holland I enjoyed the sight of fields, pretty canals, familiar-shaped Dutch roofs and neat suburban developments. I arrived in Apeldoorn at 8.45pm and it was still light. Once again I found myself disorientated. I couldn't find my way out of the station; there were lots of tunnels and no signs. The place was deserted. Suddenly a man appeared, a rather dishevelled-looking man, and he offered to help. He showed me where to get the lift up to ground level and I was very grateful. There are so many helpful people in the Netherlands. I came out of the lift on to an equally deserted platform area, looked around for a while and then caught sight of a taxi rank parked further down. Relief once more.

It was a ten-minute drive through the town to my hotel. As the taxi approached it I was entranced to see banners stretched from one side of the street to the other, all saying the same thing in English, 'Hello Again, Hello Again'. I felt welcomed. Was it too fanciful that this could have been my father talking to me yet again? I realised that this was the main street, called Loolan, which was where the main parade would take place on Friday 8th May, the actual anniversary of the liberation of the Netherlands, and my hotel, The Bastion, was at the end of it. I would not be there on the Friday as this was to be only a two-day visit, nevertheless it was exciting to be there at this auspicious time.

It was a very friendly hotel. I checked in, left my case in my room and went down to the restaurant where I enjoyed a baked salmon and a glass of white wine. On returning to my room to unpack I could not find the keys to the padlock on my case. I panicked and rushed back down to ask the receptionist if he could help. He handed me a pair of pliers which I used to grapple with the lock. After twenty minutes of nervous anxiety and profuse sweating I succeeded in twisting it open. I was both relieved and cross with myself; I had never done such a silly thing before. I realised that this had all been due to my nervousness about the following day's meeting with Fraser. I had another glass of wine and went thankfully to bed.

Wednesday 6th May

I woke late and rushed down to breakfast. It was a simple buffet but I couldn't eat very much. My nervousness had taken away my appetite. I went back up to my room, put my iPad and some photos in my bag and then phoned Fraser's hotel, The Bilderberg. The receptionist put me through to his room. His voice was very relaxed as he told me he had just entered his room in order to call me; he said we were 'on the same channel'. He had a lovely Canadian accent and did not sound at all like how I expected a ninety-year-old to sound. He told me to come round right away as he was waiting for me.

 I gathered myself together and left my hotel at 10.30am. It was only a short walk away to the Bilderberg. The road was very quiet, lined with beautiful trees, not the busy road I had expected. I approached the hotel with ever-mounting nervousness, expecting that Fraser would be sitting in the lounge and that I would have to look around for him. Not at all.

 There he stood waiting for me at the other end of the hotel foyer. He was wearing a bright red sweater. Fraser Muir. The only person in the world still alive today to have heard the last words my father had spoken as his aircraft was shot down and he had plummeted to earth seventy years previously. I walked steadily towards him along the carpet, only dimly aware that photographers were standing on either side ready to capture the moment of our meeting. As I got within hugging distance I fell into his arms while the cameras flashed and we stood locked together for many minutes, each of us with tears in our eyes and on our cheeks, scarcely able to believe that this moment had come at last.

 The photographers, full of smiles, wanted a photo of us standing together looking at the camera so, trying to gather my composure, I took off my jacket and we posed, arms around each other, in front of a mosaic backdrop. I was still very teary-eyed. They took their photos and left, saying they knew we wanted to talk to each other. One of the photographers was from Canada Remembers, part of a government organisation called Veteran Affairs Canada and it had its own page on Facebook. That memorable photo was that day posted on their page with an inscription:

Canada Remembers
Fraser Muir, a Canadian Veteran from Wasaga Beach, Ontario, enlisted in the Royal Air Force in 1943. He was serving as a member of 5 Group Royal Air Force Bomber Command, stationed in England. During a mission, Wing Commander and Master Bomber Eric Benjamin was shot

AFTERWORD

down over Germany on the night of February 19, 1945, and plunged to the ground. Mr. Muir heard his last words but it was not until years later he learned that Benjamin had lost his life that day. Many years later, he traced Jeannie Benjamin, Mr. Benjamin's daughter, through social media and they have remained in contact. This week Fraser Muir is in the Netherlands to mark the 70th anniversary of the liberation of the country. Today, for the first time, he met Jeannie.

I was still wiping away my tears as I picked up my bag and my jacket and Fraser ushered me to a quieter corner of the large lounge area. We sat down in comfy armchairs. I was feeling disorientated and somewhat lightheaded. Fraser was very calm, quiet and gentle as he began to show me photos of his family on his iPad. A little later his wife Joan came along to join us. I gradually regained my equilibrium as we all chatted over coffee and later ate some lunch together, although my appetite was still not functioning properly. I found them both to be delightful people as I learned more about their lives and their family history.

During the course of the afternoon Fraser disappeared upstairs and Joan and I carried on chatting. A little while later he reappeared in the full veteran's uniform of the Royal Canadian Air Force, complete with medals; what a dashing handsome man he looked. He was now all prepared for the recording of the video I had previously mentioned. I asked another very handsome younger man standing nearby if he would kindly operate my iPad while I interviewed Fraser about the night he heard my father's last words and he kindly obliged. I later found out that this kind man was Major Carl Gauthier, M.M.M., C.D., AdeC., of the Canadian Department of National Defence, who was in charge of the whole delegation of Canadian Veterans. After a couple of false starts, we made a recording of Fraser talking about that fateful night. I was so pleased. It is now captured for posterity on Youtube under the title, 'Fraser Muir Remembers'.

After a little while longer chatting with Joan and Fraser I decided it was time to take my leave as they were due to attend an evening engagement. I found it hard, very hard, to leave. With more tears in my eyes I gave them both lots of hugs. We said how wonderful it had been and that we could hardly believe it had happened. As I walked out through the foyer and out of the hotel I turned back to wave and they were both there, just looking. Fraser waved again and that was it.

I started to retrace my steps back to my hotel but it was raining and I didn't want to go and sit sadly in my hotel room so I took the turning to the nearby Palais Het Loo, a Royal Palace and tourist attraction. I took refuge from the rain in a lovely café within the grounds. I needed a bit of comfort in the shape of a cappuccino and a large piece of carrot cake. My appetite was beginning to return. I needed to sit and assimilate what had just occurred. In 2014 I had published my first book, *It's Not The Same Friday* and concluded it with the words: 'Perhaps the day will still come when we may meet: I could yet decide to take another trip to Canada and come face to face with the man who heard the last words my father ever spoke'.

That amazing, wonderful momentous event had now taken place. I needed to process the fact that I had just met the only person in the world who had heard my father speak his last words when he fell to his death seventy years previously. I needed to sit down and I also felt the need to have other people around me, not to be in a hotel room on my own. I was pleased to be in a busy café within the comfort of strangers.

On returning to my hotel room I found the keys to the padlock for my case, which I had been desperately looking for the previous evening. They were in full view on the other bed. A little later I went down to eat but still wasn't very hungry. I was once again having to hold back the tears as I sat at the table. It had been a truly extraordinary day. Before going to sleep I watched television to try and take my mind somewhere else. It was a programme about the following day's General Election in the UK. It helped bring me back to present day reality and I was keenly awaiting the results. I had of course previously cast my postal vote.

<u>Thursday 7th May</u>

During the whole journey home to England I was still having to fight back my tears; the emotion of the previous day kept coming over me in waves. Before I left the hotel Fraser and I had exchanged a couple of emails. I told him that I was still feeling somewhat overwhelmed by the extraordinary and momentous nature of what had happened the previous day and how happy I was that he had found me and Sally. He responded with these words:

> I too cannot convince myself that at long and at last we have met. As we say back home, 'my Wheels Are Still Spinning'. It was such a pleasure to meet you and hold you and remember your Dad, and the connection we have.....every birthday I'm sure we'll spend together in spirit.....

It was his mention of holding me that immediately brought tears to my eyes once more; it seemed to bring home to me all the physical contact that I had missed, albeit subconsciously, from my own father.

After negotiating my way home by train across the flat plains of the Netherlands to Schipol airport and then boarding my flight to London I arrived back in Reading still feeling very emotional. I phoned Sally as soon as I got home and related the whole experience in detail, once more with a

AFTERWORD

lump in my throat. She was, naturally, as touched by it as I was.

It was of course Election Day and the shock of the exit poll at 10.00pm announcing that the Conservatives, against all expectations, were set to be the largest party and that David Cameron would unfortunately remain as Prime Minister brought me back to earth and to the present day with a hefty bump.

However, my meeting with Fraser Muir was indelibly fixed in my consciousness. I felt there was now a real tangible connection with my father, whom I had scarcely known and couldn't actually remember. I had not expected to be quite so overcome by the momentousness of the occasion, nor to have such a visceral reaction which caused me to lose my appetite. A few days later there was a further email from Fraser, sent to both Sally and me:

> Our meeting was a sort of climax to a 'One in a Million' happening in my life. Somehow I knew I had to keep searching to find you two. Looking back throughout my life the memory of your Dad never left so it has given me an unbelievable amount of joy and satisfaction that my determination has paid off in spades. I sometimes actually believe that your Father's spirit has guided me and that has given him even more Peace. Sally I will make every effort to visit you my dear.

Sadly, one year later, at the age of ninety-two, Fraser Muir died. I shall be forever grateful to this very special man for bringing me to a closer connection with the father I felt I never had and whose presence I have always missed. However, as Philip Larkin says in *An Arundel Tomb*, 'What will survive of us is love'.

It was my meeting with Fraser Muir which inspired me to find out more about my father's life. I grew up knowing that my father was a hero. There was never any doubt about it. My mother, my grandparents, my aunts, uncles and cousins always spoke about him with huge love, respect, admiration and reverence. His photograph was displayed on the piano in the living room, his DFC & Bar was kept in its case in my mother's bedroom, to be brought out and shown proudly to visitors, and his commemorative scroll was hung in the hallway.

But while we all acknowledged my father's heroism with great pride it was not until 2012 that the country at large gave due recognition to him and all those other extraordinary members of Bomber Command, both living and dead, who had shown such courage against enormous odds. Sixty-seven years after the end of the Second World War at the unveiling of the Bomber Command Memorial in The Green Park, London, on the day after the eighty-eighth birthday of Fraser Muir and what would have been the ninety-third birthday of my father, a very belated tribute was paid to the tremendous bravery and skill of those who had paid the ultimate sacrifice and of those who were still living.

In December 2014 I received a further, even more belated acknowledgement of my father's heroism in the form of a Bomber Command Clasp and accompanying certificate. Although welcome, such long overdue appreciation of the enormous bravery of all those in Bomber Command came with a somewhat bittersweet tinge. It was shameful that it had taken those in positions of power almost seventy years to acknowledge this country's indebtedness to a remarkable group of young men, one of whom was Eric Benjamin. No number of medals, scrolls or certificates could ever make up for the fact that on the night of 19/20 February 1945 a brave man lost his life, the country lost a hero, a young woman lost her husband and two little girls lost their father.

On 9th April 1946 my mother had received my father's DFC & Bar from King George V1. On 9th April 2016, exactly seventy years later to the day, Fraser Muir was presented with the Légion d'Honneur. Such synchronicity is yet further indication that the two men are forever linked. Separated by five years but sharing the same birthday on 27th June, they will both always be honoured in my memory. As Fraser himself said to me, '… every birthday I'm sure we'll spend together in spirit …'.

Endnotes

1. It is interesting to learn the fates of those commissioned at the same time as Eric and sharing similar service numbers. Eric Bell (77775) was killed in a flying accident on 23 July 1940. John Bellingham (77776) survived the war and was awarded the Air Force Cross (AFC). Guy Biden (77778) was killed in action 16 May 1940 with No. 16 squadron in a Lysander over Dunkirk. He was shot down in the channel, having been intercepted looking for targets of opportunity to bomb and spotting for his own troops. Peter Billyeald (77779) completed two tours of operations in 1940/41 and 1943 and was awarded the DFC as a squadron leader with No. 464 RAAF squadron flying Lockheed Venturers. He added a Military MBE and was Mentioned in a Despatch twice. He died in 2004.
2. In response to Air Ministry Spec. P.27/32 issued three years earlier.
3. Memoirs of Group Captain Patrick Foss kept in RAF Pathfinders Archive.
4. Memoirs of Bob Pearce kept in RAF Pathfinders Archive.
5. A photograph of the damaged but otherwise intact aircraft survives, the Battle being inspected by a German Luftwaffe officer. No Luftwaffe fighter claims were made for a Fairey Battle that day. Four aircraft were claimed as shot down by units of JG2 and JG3 – two Bristol Blenheims and two Hawk 75s.
6. The Appendices of the No. 73 Squadron ORB contain a number of first-hand accounts of those last 24 hours in France.
7. They had been evacuated as part of Operation Aerial, the lifting of Allied forces from ports in western France.
8. A.H Narracott of *The Times*.
9. While it cannot be proven completely, as contemporary records and memories differ, there is a possibility that the French pilot was none other than Jean Demozay, who won fame as a fighter pilot flying under the name of Moses Morlaix. Demozay has been a liaison officer with the RAF from the beginning of the war, and attached to No. 1 Squadron, one of a handful of Hurricane squadrons then in France. Sadly, Demozay did not long survive the war, being killed in a flying accident in December 1945.
10. As quoted in *Valiant Wings* by Norman Franks, published by William Kimber, 1988.

11. As many as 7,000 people may have died in the tragedy. The ship had originally been launched as the *Tyrrhenia* in 1920 and remained the *RMS Lancastria* in 1924 and *HMT Lancastria* on the outbreak of war, having been requisitioned as a troopship.
12. The Irish lady has been identified as Mary O'Shaughnessy; the Scottish lady is identified only as 'Mrs S'. The former, who was actually from Wigan, was later arrested by the Gestapo and sent to Ravensbrück Concentration Camp.
13. AIR81/946 provides details of Hillyard's injuries and subsequent evacuation. WO 373/61/630 includes a citation for his MiD. WO208/3302/266 recounts his escape and evasion.
14. George Roskell had a similar experience to Hillyard. He'd left hospital to escape the German advance, making his way first to Angers and then on to Nantes. He was smuggled out of hospital again, when the Germans entered the town, and hidden in a convent. With his hiding placed discovered, he was officially deemed a prisoner of war, but was spirited away again and after a series of adventures was helped as far as the unoccupied zone with a plan to cross the Pyrenees into Spain. With insufficient funds with which to pay his guides, he made for Marseille, and through the American Consul was directed to the Reverend Caskie. On the 14 December he went before the Mixed Medical Board and passed for repatriation. He was presented with his MM by His Majesty the King at Buckingham Palace, 5 May 1942 and died in Chelmsford in 1981. His medals were recently sold by Noonan's at auction in October 2022.
15. *AASF* by Charles Gardner p232.
16. *The Royal Air Force 1939 – 1945* p185.
17. Carter later went on to command No. 103 Squadron and became station commander at RAF Waltham. He survived the war.
18. Spiller was later lost on operations in May 1941.
19. Charles Elliott was killed in March 1941 in a flying accident.
20. *Royal Air Force 1939-1945* vol 1 p187.
21. A Geodetic airframe is a type of construction developed by Barnes Wallis in the 1930s of a basket-weave criss-cross style pattern that gave the aircraft considerable strength. It had evolved out of the airframe design of early airships.
22. Muggeridge went on to be commissioned and win the DFC later in the war with 37 Squadron.
23. RAF 'slang' for an ambulance.
24. Later promoted squadron leader, Carlyon served with distinction with No. 150 Squadron throughout 1941, being awarded the DFC in September. Sadly he did not survive the war, being killed on the night of 15 January 1943 flying a Stirling with No. 214 Squadron. He was 31.
25. AIR81/4192.
26. Eric arrived 18 May 1941 along with Pilot Officer Ian Bonard for flying duties. Bonard was shot down and killed in April 1943 while on a minelaying trip with No. 196 Squadron.

ENDNOTES

27. Bobbington was later renamed Halfpenny Green to avoid it being confused in R/T with RAF Bovingdon in Hertfordshire.
28. To put this into context, at the start of training on 7 June 1941, nineteen aircraft were available. By the end of the day, only seven were still deemed serviceable.
29. Later Air Marshal Sir Brian Baker.
30. Later Air Vice Marshal Sir John Whitford.
31. J G Good was posted to Bobbington on 1 May 1941 from No. 53 Squadron.
32. Batten was one of four aircrew attached temporarily from Bobbington to operational stations on 27 May for the attack.
33. *Rough Landing or Fatal Flight* – Steve Poole – p61-62.
34. Rainsford was posted out on 26 October. He later went on to command No. 115 Squadron. In 1986 he published his autobiography, *Memoirs of an Accidental Airman*.
35. Bruntingthorpe is ten miles south of Leicester.
36. To be 'coned' by a searchlight is to be captured and illuminated by a searchlight's powerful beam which could easily blind and disorientate the pilot.
37. *London Gazette* 5 August 1941.
38. *Flypast* May 2015.
39. *Night Bombing* – Hector Hawton – 1944.
40. Adams was later awarded the DFC and killed in action with No. 630 Squadron on 22 June 1944.
41. Of the PFF squadrons operating that night to Pilsen, one was lost from No. 35 Squadron, and two each from No. 83 Squadron and No. 156 Squadron.
42. It went on to complete 75 operations, eventually being lost over Berlin on night of 26/27 November 1943.
43. Mattick was later awarded the DFM and killed in action on 2 January 1944.
44. Jones would also go on to be awarded the DFM.
45. *Bomber Command War Diaries*, Martin Middlebrook, p394).
46. Pearce went on to be commissioned and complete his tour. He was awarded the DFC in 1944 with No. 9 Squadron as a flight lieutenant.
47. Whereas the wives of non-commissioned officers and men were cared for at Queen Charlotte's and other large maternity hospitals, in the early stages of the war there had been no dedicated facilities for officers' wives. Fulmer Chase was reserved for wives of the three fighting services whose income did not exceed £400 per year and included many promoted from the ranks. (Letter from Clementine Churchill to Mrs Lehman dated 1 August 1941.)
48. *Night Bombing*, Hector Hawton, p62.
49. A comprehensive list is provided in Martin Middlebrook's *Berlin Raids*, Viking 1988, p22.
50. On the night of 23/24 August 1943.
51. Francis P O'Malley survived the war and remained in the RAF for some time after.
52. The attack by the two Ju88s is recorded in Say's logbook (although wrongly dated 5.9). No official combat report appears to survive at the National Archive. JB137 was repaired and was struck off charge in October 1946.

53. Edward Pullen went on to take command of No. 50 Squadron in December but his tenure was short-lived. He was shot down and killed on a raid on Frankfurt.
54. Len would later be Mentioned in Despatches, published in the *London Gazette* 8 June 1944.
55. Jimmy Moss was a talented sportsman and much-loved schoolmaster who spoke highly of his brother airmen from all parts of the Empire and America, and his great appreciation of the groundcrews who served them. A warm tribute to Moss is recounted in the Radley College archives.
56. A DFC for Greig earned during his time with No. 57 Squadron was published in a supplement to the *London Gazette* in August 1943.
57. Later Wing Commander Jerry Gosnell DSO, DFC, CO No. 571 Squadron, and Wing Commander Mike Stephens DSO, DFC & 2 Bars.
58. Believed to be Squadron Leader Douglas Frostick, later Mentioned in Despatches in 1946 and then again for operations in Malaya in 1958.
59. Eric was posted to Warboys on 4th November 1944. His corresponding arrival at RAF Warboys is not recorded in the official document, but he returned to No. 54 Base on 10th November 1944, his training complete.
60. Later Air Vice Marshal H.V.Satterly CB, CBE, DFC.
61. Woodroffe survived the war only to lose his life in a crash in Florida in 1957.
62. *London Gazette* 17 October 1944.
63. Stubbs survived the war and became a group captain with the DSO, OBE and DFC. He died at the age of 55 in 1973.
64. *At First Sight* – Alan Webb. 1991.
65. *Guy Gibson*. Richard Morris p272.
66. Source: *V Group News* No 29
67. *The Right of the Line*. John Terraine.
68. AIR 14/2437.
69. *Bomber Command War Diaries*. Middlebrook p652.
70. December 29, 1944 issue.
71. AIR29/854.
72. AIR27/2150.
73. Wing Commander R G W Oakley DSO, DFC, DFM.
74. Frank Ling, a Canadian pilot with No. 50 Squadron, was one who came below the cloud base to bomb; Squadron Leader McCracknell of No. 189 Squadron thought the good marking wasted. Several crews within 207 were adamant that a third voice ordering main Force to bomb the Greens was a spoof as it was not heard on VHF and did not use any of the agreed call signs.

Index

1 Group 20,22,47,101
11 Squadron 22
12 Operational Training Unit 10
12 Squadron 11
13 Squadron 12
16 Operational Training Unit 71
17 Operational Training Unit 71
103 Squadron 10,20,26– 27
106 Squadron 41,47,65,95
113 Squadron 66
150 Squadron 10,12–14,16,18,21,23–24,26–27,36
157 Squadron 75
158 Squadron 89
1654 Heavy Conversion Unit 89
1660 Conversion Unit 40–41,76,81,87
2 Air Navigation School 30
27 Squadron 22
29 Operational Training Unit 36–37
207 Squadron 75,88
214 Squadron 25,102
226 Squadron 20
238 Squadron 88
3 Air Observers Navigation School 32,34–35
3 Flying Instructors School 78,80
3 Group 45
3 Initial Training Wing 5
304 Squadron 47
305 Squadron 47
4 RAF Hospital 29
467 Squadron 59–60
44th Bombardment Group 67
5 Group ix,45,47,58,67,71,84,87,91,97,101,
  107–108,118,122
50 Squadron 66–68,88,89
51 Group 32
54 Base ix,85,87,95,103,110
61 Squadron 36,45–48,53,58,60,62–63,65,67,71,75,82
601 Squadron 88
605 Squadron 22
615 Squadron 22
617 Squadron 37,58
619 Squadron 88
627 Squadron 84,91–92,95,97,101,108,110
7 Service Flying Training School 5,9
76 Squadron 88
8 Group 83–84,108
83 Squadron 87,88,91,95–96,108
85 Squadron 75
9 Group 75
97 Squadron 91,95,108
98 Squadron 11–12,18

Aachen 48
Aberbeeg 3
Adams, Robert 53
Addlestone 2,114
Admiral Hipper 94
Admiral Scheer 94
Advanced Air Striking Force 10–13,20
Air Transport Auxiliary 4
Alkett factory 62
Amos, Derek 32
Amsterdam 121
Andrews, Sydney 13
Angers 19
Antwerp 24
Apeldoorn 119–121
Armstrong, Sergeant 14,23
Auschwitz 105

Baker, Brian 32
Balliol 48
Barclay, George 48
Barratt, Arthur 11,13–14,20
Barry, Claudia 3,5,8,16,18,26–29,33–35,37,39,47,52,61
Barry, Desmond ix,3,35,71,107
Barry, Sarah 3,8,71,80,105
Barry, Stephen 3,8,71,80,97–98,105,107
Barry, Winnie 3,7–8,61,70
Bartley, Tony 48
Batten, Hector 35
Baxter, Wing Commander 83
Beale, Flight Lieutenant 13
Benjamin, Albert 1,2,18
Benjamin, Arthur 2,114
Benjamin, Beatrice 1,71
Benjamin, Betty vii – ix,3–5,7–9,16–18,21,26–33,
  36–38,41,45,52,54,61,64,70–74,78–80,
  82–83,85,93,96,98–99,102–107,110,112–113,
  115–116
Benjamin, Ernest 1,2,114
Benjamin, Jeannie 39,61–62,71,80,83,93,99–102,
  114–115,123

Benjamin, Leslie 1,2,113–114
Benjamin, Levina 114
Benjamin, Maud 113–114
Benjamin, Moses 1
Benjamin, Sally 105–106,114–115,117,119,124–125
Benjamin, Victoria (Queenie) 1–2,98–99
Bennett, Donald 84
Benson 9–10
Berchtesgaden 3
Berlin 49,62,67–69,76,89,107,115,118,120
Bilderberg hotel 122
Bismarck 94
Blackburn 89
Blagdon, Reginald 67
Bléré 20
Blom, Walter 21
Blore, H F 67
BMW factory 62
Bobbington 32,73,82
Böhlen 108,113,118–119
Bomber Command Memorial 117–119,125
Boulogne 23–24
Bournemouth 8
Bradley, Robert 13
Breen, John 22
Bremen 87
Bridgnorth 33
Brill, Charles 45
Bristol 78
British Air Forces in France 11
Brooke-Popham, Robert 36
Brown, Eric 47
Bruntingthorpe 37
Brux 101–102,104–105,108
Buckingham Palace 114
Burke 92
Burrows, Robert 13
Bushy Park 3

Calais 23–24
Callaway, William 45
Cameron, David 125
Carter, Robert 22–23
Carylon, Paul 26–27
Caskie, Reverend 20
Chamberlain, Neville 3–4,8
Charlottenburg 115–116
Cheddar Gorge 79
Chemnitz 107
Cheshire, Leonard 84
Chester, Albert 32
Churcher, Ronnie 92,95
Churchill, Winston 16,22,36
Cincinnati 48
Clark, John 40
Clemenceau, Georges 1
Coad, Richard 48
Cochrane, Ralph 58,84,88,91,102
Cockington 30
Colditz 110,113,115
Cologne 34,89
Coningsby ix,87,96–97,100,104–105,107
Constantine, Hugh 102
Corr, Duncan 46
Cottesmore 27
County Cork 3
Cousens, Bryce 65
Cranage 30

Cranwell 22,29
Crawshaw, William 56
Crespigny, Claude De 45
Crewe 35
Crofts, Peter 22
Cross, Fred 29
Curry, George 95

Daimler Benz 62
Danville 14
Daytona Beach 57
Derby 88
Dickens, Charles 37
Dierkes, William 48–49,51–52
Dinsdale, Richard 40,71
Dobrany 54
Dornier factory 62
Dortmund 57
Douglas 35
Dresden ix,107
Dreuz 15
Duisberg 51,57
Dundas, Hugh 48
Dundas, John 48
Dunkirk 13
Düsseldorf 57,66

East Bridgeford 21
Ecury-sur-Coole 13
Edinburgh 47
Elliott, Charles 14,23
Elsham Wolds 102
Emden 94,97
Enville 32–33,35
Erfurt 108
Essen 57
Evans, Charlotte 115
Evans, Dylan 115
Evreux 14

Fauquier, Johnny 63
Feltwell 35
Figg, Henry 13
Finlay, Don 22
Finningley 88
Fisher, Reverend 32,36
Flushing 24
Foulsham 90
Frank, Alan 18
Frankfurt 51,90–91
Frawley, Joseph 41,63
Friedrichshafen 58
Frisian Islands 45
Frostick, Douglas 80
Fulmer Chase 61

Garvey, Frederick 80
Gascoyne-Cecil, Rupert 48,53–54,57,63
Gaulle, Charles de 16
Gauthier, Carl 123
Gelsenkirchen 60
Genoa 50
Gibraltar 20
Gibson, Guy 47,58,84–85,92
Giessen 91–92
Gneisenau 94
Gomm, Cosme 59
Good, Johnny 33
Göring, Hermann 5,22

INDEX

Gosnell, Jerry 80
Green Park, The 117,125
Greenock 20
Greig, John 76
Guderian, General 64
Gurney, Sarah 3
Gydnia 97

Hadler, Rebecca 115
Hadler, Toby 115
Halfpenny Green 32
Hall, Geoffrey 48,51–52
Halton 30
Hamburg 60
Hampton 1–3
Hampton Grammar School 1
Hampton Hill Sea Scouts 2
Hanover 69,90
Harris, Arthur 34,46,53,56,58,62,69,
    83–84,90,102,105,107–108
Hawker Aircraft 1
Hearn, Edward 90
Heath, Jack 89,91,97,113,115
Heathrow 120
Heilbronn 91
Helsby, Derek 77
Helt, Radovan 102
Hemswell 45
Hendon 18,25,96
Henschel factory 62
Her Majesty the Queen 117
Hereford 3
Hesketh, Allen 12,74,102–103,112
Heston 4
Hewitt, Len 40,52,69,101
High Wycombe 107
Hillyard, Eric 14–15,19–20
Hitler, Adolf 3
Honey, Aubrey 7
Horten 97
Houssay 13
Huntingdon 6,96

Ingham, Charles 61
Ingham, John 95
Ingram, Norman 13
Isle of Man 35
Isle of Wight 4
Jaywick Sands 4
Jenkins, Robert 12
Johnson, Peter 95
Jones, Thomas 57

Kassel 65
Kelly, Ernest 40
King George VI 126
Kingston 1
Kinloss 95–96
Koln 94–97
Koltzschen 110

L'hopital Michel Lévy
La Ferté-Vidame 15
Lancastria 18
La Pallice 89,94
La Rochelle 89
La Spezia 53,56,60
Lake Constance 58

Larkin, Philip 125
Le Creusot 46,58
Le Mans 13,15,19
Leigh, Sergeant 23
Leipzig 90,107–108,113,118
Leuna 91
Light Night Striking Force 108
Lincoln 45,82,96
Lissett 90
Lloyd George, David 1
Loches 20
Lock, Alf 5–6,16,18,26–29,33–35,37,39,46
London 17,18,22–23,45,79,81,96,124
London Gazette 48,64
London Universal Insurance Company 2
Long, Mrs 112
Lossiemouth 96
Lough Neagh 11
Louvieres 14
Lulsgate Bottom 78,81

Maastricht 11
MacFarlane 54
Madrid 20
Maison Blanche 58,59
Manchester 77
Marseille 20
Marshalls 35
Mattick, Stan 57
McIndoe, Archibald 22
Mellor 89
Metheringham 84,104
Milan 49–50
Milltown 95
Mortin Hall 108
Moss 97
Moss, E H 69,73
Muggeridge, Charles 27
Muir, Fraser 109,117–120,122–126
Muir, Joan 123
Munich 4,65,97
Munro, Les 36

Nantes 14–17
Neary, Edward 77
Newark 52
Newton 19,20,21,26,77 78
Nocton Hall 29
North Killingholme 77
North Luffenham 36–37,39
Nottingham 6,19,27,30,77
Nuremberg 73

O'Malley, Frank 63
Oakley, Rupert 109–110
Odbert, Reginald
Orlando, Vittoria 1
Orleans 13
Oslofjord 94,97–98
Osnabruck 91
Otmoor 11
Oxford 48

Paignton 29
Pakenham, Raymond 32
Palais Het Loo 123
Pathfinders 46,51,53–57,63,67,80,83–84,87–88,92,
    95–96,108

Peacock-Edwards, Spencer 22
Pearce, David 60
Peenemünde 62
Penman, William 47–48,60,63–64
Peterborough ix,5,96,107
Peterhead 95,97
Petty, George 88,97
Pilsen 53,56–57,63
Playfair, 'Pip' 12,20
Pointon, Frank 90
Politz 97,101,105
Possington Park Hotel 8
Pouan-les-Vallées 12–13
Primley Zoo 29
Prinz Eugen 94
Pullen, Squadron Leader 68
Purdon, Peter 32

Radley 69
Rafter, Charles 26
Rainsford, Freddie 37
Rankin, Herbert 53
Raphael, Alfred 60
Rauceby 29
Reading 117,120,124
Reid, Bill 66–67
Rheinhausen 51
Ridge, Fred 115–116
Rijksmuseum 121
Rogers, Rich 80
Root-Reed, Maurice 40,53,63,65,67
Rose, Hilyer 2,114
Roskell, George 20
Rossignol, James 57
Royal High School 47
Runnymede memorial 115

Sachsenhausen 101
Sale 77
Samlesbury 115
Satterly, Harry 87,110–112
Saundby, Robert 108
Say, Leonard 63–64
Scampton 71,74,81
Scharnhorst 94
Schiphol 121,124
Schneider Factory 46
Scott, Walter 47
Sedan 11–12
Sharp, Alfred 87
Shipdham 67
Shipley 4
Shortt, Harry 90
Shrewsbury 77
Siemens 62,64
Sinclair, Archibald 24
Skellingthorpe 65,67,72,90
Skoda Factory 54
Slee, Leonard 58
Smith, Maurice 88,107
Snaith 36
Sobieski 20
Spandau 62
Speer, Albert 102
Spence, Arthur 77
Spezia 50
Spiller, Victor 23
St Albans 3

St Leonards-on-Sea 5
St Nazaire 14,18
Stamford 33,36
Steed, Frederick 40,71
Stephens, Mike 80
Stephenson, Ken 41,65,67
Stettin 56
Stewart, Thomas 62
Steyning 115
Stidolph, Reginald 65–68
Stoke Poges 61
Stoughton 114
Stourbridge 32
Stowe 48
Stradishall 18,20,25–26
Stroud, George 22
Stubbs, Cecil 89
Stubbs, Dennis 85,88–89,97,106
Stubbs, Robert 89
Stubbs, Stanley 89
Sutton Bridge 35
Swinderby 40–41,73–74,76–78,81,89,106
Syerston 47–49,52,57,65,72

Taaffe, Rudolph 36
Tain 95–96
Teddington 3,7,17,36,61,72
Tirpitz 94
Torquay 29,30
Tours 13,19
Treaty of Versailles 1
Trenchard, Lord 103–104
Turner, Alec 2
Turner, Joan 2,98
Turner, Sylvia 2,98
Twickenham 61

Vereinigte Stahlwerke 51
Vernon 14
Viry 14

Waddington 41
Wadham College 88
Wainfleet 58
Wallingford 9
Wallis, Barnes 36
Warboys 84–85,94
Wasaga Beach 122
Wellburn, Dennis 62
Weybridge 2
Wheeler, Vashon 75
White Waltham 4
Whitford, John 32
Wilhelmshaven 94
Wilkie, 'Jimmy' 89–90
Wilkinson, Stanley 90
Williams, Gwilym 77
Wilson, Woodrow 1
Wimsett, Arthur 95
Windsor (Ontario) 48
Winnipeg 114
Woodhall Spa 84,108
Woodroofe, John 87–88,95,97
Woodvine, Arthur 67
Woolfox Lodge 47
Wuppertal 57

Yaeldon, Percy 2